WITHDRAWN

Algarve

~~WITHDRAWN~~

WITHDRAWN

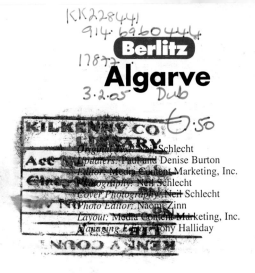

Berlitz

Algarve

Original Text: Neil Schlecht
Updaters: Paul and Denise Burton
Editor: Media Content Marketing, Inc.
Photography: Neil Schlecht
Cover Photography: Neil Schlecht
Photo Editor: Naomi Zinn
Layout: Media Content Marketing, Inc.
Managing Editor: Tony Halliday

Second Edition 2003 (Reprinted 2004)

NO part of this book may be reproduced, stored in a retrieval system or transmitted in any form or means electronic, mechanical, photocopying, recording or otherwise, without prior written permission from Apa Publications. Brief text quotations with use of photographs are exempted for book review purposes only.

CONTACTING THE EDITORS
Every effort has been made to provide accurate information in this publication, but changes are inevitable. The publisher cannot be responsible for any resulting loss, inconvenience or injury. We would appreciate it if readers would call our attention to any errors or outdated information by contacting Berlitz Publishing, PO Box 7910, London SE1 1WE, England. Fax: (44) 20 7403 0290;
e-mail: berlitz@apaguide.co.uk; www.berlitzpublishing.com

CONTENTS

● A ( in the text denotes a highly recommended sight

Algarve

THE ALGARVE AND ITS PEOPLE

For much of the world, the Algarve is synonymous with Portugal, yet the Portuguese will tell you the exact opposite: the region has little in common with the rest of the country. The southern stretch of coast is more reminiscent of a North African landscape than a European one. It has no cosmopolitan cities, such as Lisbon and Porto, which are farther north. Most of Portugal is known for quaint towns, medieval castles, and grand palaces. The Algarve is more recognizable for impenetrable blocks of tourist apartments, hotels, and meticulously manicured golf courses.

And beaches. Think Algarve and the mind pictures long, glorious stretches of golden sands, secluded coves framed by odd ochre-coloured rock formations, and deep green waters. With about 160 km (100 miles) of coastline, Portugal's southern province is one of Europe's premier beach destinations. The occasionally chilly ocean is the Atlantic, but the Algarve has a sultry Mediterranean feel.

Its consistent climate is the best in Portugal, and one of the kindest in the world: more than 250 days of sunshine a year – more than almost any other international resort area. The moderating effect of the Gulf Stream produces a fresh springtime breeze throughout winter, and in late January and February, white almond blossoms blanket the fields. In summer the heat is intense but rarely unbearable, and regardless, beautiful beaches and innumerable pools are always just a drive away.

Magnificent year-round weather has made the Algarve a huge destination for sporting holidays. Superb golf facilities abound – several with tees dramatically clinging to cliffs and fairways just skirting the edge of the ocean – and horseback riding, tennis, big-game fishing, sailing and windsurfing are immensely popular.

Sports, beaches and hospitable weather – not to mention easily organized package holidays – are surely the reasons that the Algarve receives as many visitors as the rest of Portugal in its entirety. But it's not just international tourists that descend on the Algarve; many Portuguese from Lisbon and elsewhere in the north have holiday homes and spend their summer holidays here.

The coast is neatly divided into the rugged Barlavento to the west and the flat beauty of Sotavento to the east. West is where you'll find the famous orange cliffs and surreal eroded rock stacks. Near Cabo de São Vicente and Sagres, the extreme western point, the terrain is surprisingly barren and the facilities decidedly low-key. The ocean can also be forbiddingly cold.

Tourist resorts clutter the entire middle of the coast, from Lagos to Faro, with a spectrum of homes away from home – monster high-rises to spacious, single-storey villas – spilling across the rolling hills and lining the beaches. Resorts such as Portimão, Albufeira and Vilamoura would appear to have little room left to grow, yet tourist facilities seem to mate with each other and reproduce overnight. Much of the unstoppable growth is crass and frighteningly commercial, and the crowds in summer unbearable.

The eastern third of the Algarve is a more sedate marriage of coast and ocean, with warm waters and hot sands stretching past the wetlands of Ria Formosa to the Spanish border. The Algarve's most picturesque town, Tavira, is along this section of the coast.

Away from the coast, the terrain slopes through pines, mimosa, eucalyptus, and heather to an altitude of nearly 915 m (3,000 ft). Holidaymakers wishing to escape the maddening beach crowds can run for the hills, especially the tantalizing Serra de Monchique.

The region's exotic name is derived from the Arabic, Al-Gharb, meaning 'country of the west'. The westernmost territory of Europe was highly prized by North African Moors, who occupied it from the eighth to the 13th centuries. Their half millennium here left indelible traces, seen today in whitewashed houses, hilltop castles and colourful ceramic tiles.

Following the Reconquest of Iberia by Christians, the Algarve led Portugal to glory and fortune. Prince Henry the Navigator established his legendary Navigation School along Portugal's southern coast (financing expeditions with royalties from the Algarve fishing industry), and intrepid explorers set out in caravels from Lagos and Sagres. In the 15th and 16th centuries, they ushered in an Age of Discovery, rounding Africa's Cape of Good Hope and eventually reaching India and the Pacific. Others found their way to the Americas and Brazil.

Opening world trade routes across the globe, they established Portugal as a maritime superpower. Spices, gold and diamonds flowed across the seas to Lisbon.

Portugal soon lapsed into decline, though, tattered by wars and constitutional crises, and for two centuries or more the Algarve remained isolated

Fishermen in Sagres port examine the day's catch with a stoic anticipation.

The Church of Santa Maria forms the backdrop for a café in Praça Dom Henrique.

from the rest of Europe. Even though the coast received many illustrious visitors from Roman times through the Middle Ages and up to the Edwardian period (when travellers came to luxuriate in Monchique's spa waters), the Algarve's elite holiday status is a relatively recent phenomenon. The first resort on the coast, Praia da Rocha, was only 'discovered' in the 1930s, and the real build-up didn't kick into overdrive until the beginning of the 1980s.

Spain's Costa del Sol developed earlier and more rapidly (and some would say, more disastrously). Yet the lessons of rampant, ill-advised development across the border were not heeded. Only recently has environmental and aesthetic consciousness at least mandated that newer developments are limited in height.

Yet – quite remarkably, in the face of the ongoing tourism onslaught – parts of the Algarve retain their old-fashioned charm. The main road along the coast, EN-125, is lined with ceramic shops and stifled with summertime traffic, but the agricultural countryside to the north is a different world. Flowering orchards and gentle grain fields replace hotels, apartments and snack bars. A slow, rural lifestyle perseveres against the rush of modern life.

For centuries, fishing has been the Algarve's lifeblood. Small fishing villages preserve their simple and unaffected ways, seemingly oblivious to the tourist hordes. Scrappy crews of small hand-painted boats troll the waters just offshore, and trawlers fish deep in the Atlantic for big shoals of *bacalhau* (cod), which is beloved by the Portuguese.

A visit to the local fish market is a revealing window into Algarvian life. Negotiations are serious but friendly. The same scenario is played out a thousand times a day at markets all across the region; every town has a market day at least once a month. Farmers bring their livestock to trade, and artisans and itinerant vendors sell their wares.

Not a large area, the Algarve is relatively easy to get around, whether by train or car (an effort that is much more relaxing outside of the main summer season). The distances between mega-resorts and unspoiled villages are surprisingly small.

Besides beaches, the Algarve's major attractions are towns that have lived through centuries of triumph and disaster. Faro, Tavira and Lagos are towns with a strong Moorish influence, and quiet mountain towns including Silves, Alte, and Salir are reminders of the days before golf courses and hotel chains.

Despite the region's ancient roots, few historic monuments survive from before 1755, when the Algarve was rocked by a monumental earthquake that took thousands of lives and levelled buildings as far north as Lisbon. Still, you'll find vestiges of a vibrant past, including evocative castle ruins and churches with extraordinary displays of Portuguese glazed tiles. Even the humblest village has a classic white church, a sleepy plaza shaded by vivid purple jacaranda, and, if you time it right, the drama of the local market.

The Portuguese are famously hospitable, if reserved. And they remain to   w that their lovely co

A BRIEF HISTORY

Little is known of the earliest Stone Age inhabitants of Europe's southwestern extremity. The ancient Greeks called them the Cynetes (or Cunetes). Whatever their origins, their culture evolved under the pressure and influence of foreign forces. Among the many invading armies that settled here and contributed to nascent Portuguese culture were Phoenicians, who settled in the area around 1,000 BC, followed by the Celts, Iberians, Greeks and Carthaginians.

But it was the Romans, who arrived late in the third century BC, who most greatly influenced all of Iberia. They built towns, industries, roads and bridges, developed agriculture, and bequeathed the Latin language, of which Portuguese is a direct descendant. The Romans named the southwestern province of the peninsula Lusitania, oddly enough for one of the Celtiberian tribes they defeated, and by the third century AD had introduced Christianity. By the beginning of the fourth century the Algarve had a bishop in place, based in Faro. But Rome had already fallen into decay, and soon hordes of northern tribesmen took over the empire. The Algarve fell to the Visigoths in the mid-fifth century.

Under Moorish Rule

In AD 711, the Moors brought powerful armies from North Africa and launched a devastating attack on the Iberian peninsula, conquering much of what would become Spain and Portugal. They imposed Islam and left an indelible influence on the countryside and the population of the Algarve. The Moorish legacy can still be seen in the form of wells and waterwheels, squat white houses, the dark complexions of the people and in the very name given the region – taken from Al-Gharb, which means 'country of the west' (when the Moors conquered the territory, it was the most westerly in the known world).

The Moors governed their Iberian kingdoms from across the border in Seville, but the Algarve had its own regional capital and huge, invulnerable fortress. The capital was Chelb (or Xelb), and it was bigger and better defended than Lisbon. Today the town, known as Silves *(see page 38)*, is a provincial outpost whose only besiegers are busloads of tourists who climb the narrow streets up to the old Moorish ramparts.

The long struggle by Christians to expel the Moors (a campaign known as the *Reconquista*, or Reconquest) began towards the end of the eighth century AD. By the 11th century, Portucale consisted of a small section of Castile and León (today's northern Portugal). Yet it wasn't until the 12th century that significant gains were made to take back southern Iberia. The beginning of the end came in the Battle of Ourique in 1139. After the victory, Count Afonso Henriques proclaimed himself the first king of Portugal, making it one of the first nation-states in Europe.

The Reconquest of Silves, not achieved for another 50 years, was a grisly affair. A mixed bag of Crusaders from northern Europe were recruited en route to their battles east in the Holy Land. They sailed upon the river port of Silves and, ignoring conditional offers of surrender, slew all the inhabitants (at no small loss to themselves) and pillaged the great treasures of the city.

Two years later Muslim forces rallied again, retaking Silves, and the Reconquista stumbled on for another half century. So many inter-religious alliances reigned, and so pervasive was the intermingling of Moors and Christians, that it was hard to tell who was on which side and for which piece of land they were fighting. On top of that, the situation was further clouded by a feud between Portugal and Spain, each of them claiming sovereignty over the Algarve. However, by 1249 Faro and the western Algarve were retaken under King Afonso III, completing the Reconquest. The possibility of war with Spain was averted by an expeditious royal marriage, and by the end of the century a treaty with Spain drew up the boundaries of Portugal that stand today.

The Algarve was a region regarded separately within the new Portugal, as is evidenced by the royal title 'Kingdom of Portugal and the Algarve'. In those days, the notion of the Algarve as a distinct entity did make some sense: like an island, it was cut off to the south and west by the Atlantic, to the east by the Guadiana River, and to the north by the mountains. The region's titular autonomy was upheld until 1910, when the monarchy itself was overthrown.

This image of the Tower of Belem at sunset is symbolic of Portugal's strong connection with the sea.

The Navigator

In 1415, long after the Reconquista was completed, a Portuguese fleet assembled on the River Tagus in Lisbon, ready for an assault on the Moors in their homeland. Crossing the Straits of Gibraltar, the armada attacked and seized the North African city of Ceuta. An illustrious member of the famous raid was the young Prince Henry – half Portuguese and half English – and the son of King João I and his wife, Philippa of Lancaster. Ceuta would be Henry's one and only military victory, though he was destined to establish Portugal as a major world power, helping to develop important world trade routes by the time of his death in 1460.

At the age of 21, Henry assembled a School of Navigation. It was certainly not a formal institution of lectures and classes, but probably resembled an informal modern-day 'think-tank.' Prince Henry – made governor of the Algarve in 1418 – had the money, influence, enthusiasm, and vision to lead and cajole the best astronomers, cartographers, boat-designers and seamen of the day to expand Portugal's maritime horizons.

The waters at the western extreme of the Algarve were all that was known to sailors. Once they were beyond Cabo de São Vicente, they faced the unknown, with no communications and no possibility of rescue if the voyage turned out badly. Yet out into the unknown they went; for the glory of God and country, and in search of personal fame and fortune. Their mission was made easier by the craft Algarve shipwrights had developed, a successor to the lumbering ships of the day: the caravel. It was light, fast and very maneuverable. Any breeze was enough for a captain to steer it where he wanted to go. With the subsequent development of new navigational techniques, it was no longer necessary

Windmills, jutting out along the coast north of Cabo de São Vicente, harness breezes coming in from the shore.

to stay within sight of land. Now the only limits to maritime exploration were man's ingenuity and courage.

According to tradition, the site of Prince Henry's base was the Sagres peninsula *(see page 22)*, though there is little there today to persuade you of this. The actual headquarters of the Navigation School may have been 40 km (25 miles) east, in Lagos *(see page 26)*. This location had a port, shipyards and was home to the prince in his role as governor of the Algarve.

During Henry's lifetime, Portugal's caravels sailed beyond the most westerly point of Africa. They colonized the Atlantic islands of Madeira and the Azores, laying the foundations for the future Portuguese empire. Before the century was over, Henry's compatriots Bartolomeu Dias and Vasco da Gama completed epic voyages, rounding the Cape of Good Hope and reaching India, respectively, and Pedro Álves Cabral claimed Brazil. Between 1519 and 1522 another Portuguese explorer, Ferdinand Magellan, led the first expedition to circumnavigate the world. Mercantilist Portugal became a rich maritime superpower.

Foreign Intrigues

To protect its seagoing interests and trade routes, Portugal established strategic garrisons in Goa (India), Malacca (East Indies), and Hormuz in the Persian Gulf. Portuguese explorers then embarked upon Macau (now Macao), the Congo and various other parts of Africa, including the Sudan. The Portuguese policy was to avoid armed strife and to develop a trade empire, rather than to conquer nations. To this end it succeeded with relatively few blood-soaked episodes in its colonial history.

Adventures abroad, however, proved disastrous during the second half of the 16th century. In 1557 the 14-year-old boy-king Sebastião ascended the throne, the beginning of a calamitous reign that was to end at the battle of Alcacer-Quiber (Morocco) in pursuit of a vain crusade. Sebastião's untimely demise, alongside some 18,000 ill-prepared, badly led followers, set the stage for a crisis of succession. For many years afterwards, legends and rumours bizarrely insisted that the king was still alive, and imposters turned up from time to time claiming the throne; those who were plausible enough to be deemed a threat were summarily executed.

In fact, the only rightful claimant to the crown was the elderly Prince Henry. But after two years of alternating between the throne and his sickbed, he died, heirless. Surveying the situation and smelling an opportunity, Spain occupied the power vacuum, and Portugal's neighbour and long-time antagonist became its master.

Spanish rule dictated Portugal's inadvertent involvement in Spain's ongoing wars. In 1587 a squadron of British ships commanded by Francis Drake attacked the Algarve (now a 'legitimate target' as Spanish territory) and sacked Sagres, thus depriving the world of the relics of Henry the Navigator. Nine years later Faro was torched. The 1386 Treaty of Windsor, by which Britain and Portugal had pledged eternal friendship, seemed a distant memory.

Portugal's empire was gradually eroded, and many of its trading posts (with the notable exception of Brazil) were picked off by the British and Dutch. Finally, after 60 years of Spanish rule, Portuguese noblemen (aided by the French, then at war with Spain) organized a palace coup and restored independence.

The Great Disaster

Portugal's greatest misfortune struck on All Saint's Day, 1 November 1755. With the candlelit churches crowded with worshippers, a monstrous earthquake struck, followed by fast-spreading fires and a devastating tidal wave that swept over the Algarve inland as far as 6.5 km (4 miles). The exact casualty figure will never be known, but it is estimated that 5,000 died immediately and between 40,000 and 60,000 perished as a result of secondary injuries and the ensuing famine and pestilence. The epicentre of the earthquake is thought to have been off the Algarve coast, possibly between Tavira and Faro, but it devastated places as far away as the capital, Lisbon. Witnesses claim to have seen a fiery volcano erupt from beneath the sea just before the first jolt.

Throughout the Algarve and much of the rest of southern Portugal, virtually every important monument, cathedral, castle, and mansion was destroyed, or at least critically damaged in the earthquake. Among the hardest hit towns was Lagos *(see page 26)* which lost its castle, its churches, and the palace in which Henry the Navigator had once lived.

Political Upheaval

The beginning of the 19th century brought further alarm to the country. This time the epicentre was Paris, and the cause of the problems, Napoleon. Just as Portugal's forced alliance with Spain had made the country a target for Drake's 16th-century raids, now her friendly alliance with England rankled Napoleon.

In 1807 the French invaded Lisbon, causing the royal family to flee to Brazil. Spain, followed by Portugal, rose up against the French occupation, in what came to be known as the Peninsular War.

Among the early blows struck for independence was a rebellion in the town of Olhão *(see page 57)*. On 16 June 1808, the townsfolk – armed with little more than ancient swords, spears and stones – attacked and captured the local French garrison. It's said that a party of local men then set sail from Olhão all the way to Brazil, without maps or navigational aids, to tell the king of the insurrection. The real battle, however, was waged under the leadership of the Duke of Wellington, whose coalition forces expelled the French after two years of bitter fighting.

The war left Portugal further weakened, and in 1822 its major empire outpost, Brazil, declared independence. At the same time, a dispute over the crown continually raged between Pedro IV, the absentee monarch who preferred to reign as Emperor of Brazil rather than return to Portugal, and his brother Miguel. The power struggle, with strong overtones of absolutism versus liberalism, excited the interest and intervention of other powers. With British help, Pedro defeated Miguel off Cape St. Vincent in 1833, and his expeditionary force marched to Lisbon. Pedro took the throne, though armed struggle continued for months and the lingering bitterness long after that.

By 1892 Portugal, racked by wars and the continuing expense of maintaining its African colonies (including those of Mozambique and Angola), declared itself bankrupt. The seeds of discontent with absolutist rule were sown.

Kingdom's End

Bloodshed would haunt the remaining years of the Portuguese monarchy. On 1 February 1908, the royal family was riding in an open carriage along the Lisbon river front plaza, Terreiro do Paço, when an assassin opened fire and killed King Carlos and the heir to the throne, Prince Luis Filipe. The prince's younger brother, Prince Manuel, was also hit, but he survived and was thus propelled to the throne at the tender age of 19.

Amid republican agitation, a surprise uprising led by elements within the armed forces deposed Manuel in 1910. Having ruled for less than three years, Manuel died in exile in 1932 in England.

The sudden end of more than seven centuries of monarchy brought confusion and crisis to the country. Presidents and prime ministers were ushered into and out of office an unbelievable 45 times between 1910 and 1926, until a military revolution suspended Portugal's problematic democracy. After six years of power, General Oscar Carmona appointed his finance minister, António de Oliveira Salazar, to be Prime Minister, a position he was to hold until 1968. Salazar's repressive rule and austerity measures rid the Portuguese economy of debt, though poverty increased. Portugal remained neutral during World War II, and Salazar demonstrated his financial acumen by selling materials and supplies to both sides.

In 1968 the elderly Salazar was forced into retirement after a stroke. His successor, Dr Marcelo Caetano, feeling the spirit of the age, began tentative relaxations of the old regime. The armed forces finally overthrew him in a popular bloodless coup, known as the 'Carnation Revolution', on 25 April 1974.

Portugal finally began to pull itself out of the long and fruitless struggle against revolutionaries in its African colonies, and granted independence to the remaining members of its empire in 1975. This, too, caused major upheavals, and a million permanent refugees rushed the motherland, aggravating the shortage of housing and jobs.

Tavira's castle looks out over the rooftops of the casco histórico (old quarter).

Although economic problems continued to beset the young democracy, the political scene was greatly stabilized. In 1986 Portugal, the former poor backwater of Europe, joined the European Economic Community (now the European Union, or EU).

With aid from the EU, Portugal became one of the fastest-growing countries in Europe. The Algarve, already a favourite of sun-seeking beach lovers from England and Northern Europe, also benefited from EU funds to build up its infrastructure and to invest in tourism. In 1998 Portugal hosted the World Expo in Lisbon. In January 2000 it was among the first group of EU members to enter the single currency, with the euro introduced as its sole unit of currency since 2002. In 2004 the country will host the European Football Championships.

WHERE TO GO

The Algarve stretches from the Atlantic Ocean to Spain, but it's actually a small region. Faro, the capital, is just 50 km (30 miles) from the Spanish border, and it is only 112 km (70 miles) west of what was known in medieval times as *o fim do mundo* (the end of the world) at Sagres. Along this 160-km (100-mile) coastal strip, resorts and holiday villages of all types have sprung up, so wherever you are based, you'll never be far from a good beach, a reasonably sized town, village, or resort, shops and nightlife.

The following pages cover the Algarve travelling west to east, though you could certainly do the reverse or begin in the centre, near Faro (or anywhere you elect to stay) and embark on day trips both east and west from there. For those with additional time and interest in seeing more of Portugal, a brief section on the Portuguese capital Lisbon and its seductive environs is included. Lisbon is about two to three hours by car (and 40 minutes by plane) from Faro; it should be conceived as an add-on to your visit to the Algarve rather than a day trip. Many people visit the Algarve by flying into Lisbon and driving to the southern coast. If you are flying directly to the international airport at Faro and wish to spend a few days in the Lisbon area, it would make sense to see about a return flight from there.

WORLD'S END:
Sagres and Cabo de São Vicente

If you begin your journey at **Sagres,** you may be in for a shock. The stark town and area around it scarcely look the part of a fabled beach resort with a Mediterranean feel. Rather, it is remote, rugged and desert-like, with only a relative smattering (compared to the rest of the Algarve) of hotels, restaurants and other facilities aimed at tourists. It is like the Algarve's outpost, which is precisely why it has so many admirers.

Sagres's connections to the sea, and Portugal's maritime exploits, are strong. Prince Henry the Navigator established his Navigation School here (though some protest that it was further east, near Lagos). The town has a picturesque working harbour, where small, brightly painted fishing boats bob and larger vessels haul in daily catches of lobster, eel and mackerel. A couple of restaurants are clustered around the harbour, with impressive views. Inland, a cute little square, Praça República, is ringed by informal (and, in summer, heaving) nightspots.

The best beaches near Sagres are sheltered and not over-crowded. **Mareta**, down below the government pousada, is the most popular. **Martinhal**, just east of the harbour, is a

The port at Sagres is constantly filled with the comings and goings of all manner of water vessels.

wide, curved beach with a first-class watersports centre. **Beliche** (also written Belixe) is a sandy expanse protected by the Cape of St Vincent. **Tonel**, just before Beliche, and **Telheiro**, about 9 km (6 miles) up the west coast from Sagres, are also well-regarded beach spots.

Beyond the village of Sagres, a great, rocky peninsula hangs above a brooding ocean. You'll understand why, in the days before the great Portuguese explorers set out from here seeking to discover the great beyond, it was known as the End of the World. Those wishing to put a positive spin on things called it Sacrum Saturni – Holy Promontory – and believed that the gods slept here.

Two beachgoers enjoy a stroll at Mareta, a popular spot for locals and tourists.

Since time immemorial this forlorn place has stirred the imagination. It shook Henry and his sailors, who are said to have set up camp at the **Fortaleza de Sagres** (Fortress) that sits on the promontory. Unfortunately, not much of the original has survived. Most of it is a 17th-century fort that was insensitively restored. In 1991, the walls of this nationally important monument were resurfaced with grey concrete, masking the external character of the building. The fortress's principal building, which may have been Henry's head-quarters, no longer exists. What you'll find inside is a small

16th-century chapel, Nossa Senhora da Graça, and what looks to be a huge stone sun dial, known as the **Rosa dos Ventos** (Rose Compass). Whether, in fact, it was a wind compass useful in the great voyages is unknown. A modern shell on the fort's grounds houses an exhibition area.

A couple of km (one mile) west of Sagres are the more authentic remains of another fortress, **Fortaleza do Beliche**. This small, attractive 17th-century castle houses a white, domed chapel (Santa Catarina) and is home to a smart traditional-style restaurant and a small annex to the pousada in Sagres. Both the fort and chapel, however, threaten to collapse because the surrounding cliffs are eroding at a frightening rate. Efforts to shore up the cliffs and save the historic site have recently been undertaken.

The windswept cliffs of **Cabo de São Vicente**, the most southwesterly point in Europe, were once surely even more bleak than they are today, when supertankers and small yachts heave into view around the cape. But even on the calmest of days, the Atlantic thunders below and the wind whips around the cape. At the tip of the point, the lighthouse, built in 1904 on the site of a convent chapel, has a beam visible up to 96 km (60 miles) away. Visitors can climb the stairs to a hot, enclosed lookout.

Visitors to Cabo de São Vicente rarely leave without making new friends.

The first settlement of any size outside Sagres is **Vila do Bispo**, 7 km (4 miles) to the north. Take a break in the peaceful town's pleasant, flower-filled garden square and pay a visit to the 18th-century parish church. The walls are covered with *azulejos* and its ceiling decorated with frescoes.

Henry the Navigator – Infante Dom Henrique – was bequeathed the land around Sagres in 1443 by his brother. Henry lived within the castle and died in Sagres in 1460, though his remains were later transferred to the Batalha monastery north of Lisbon.

About halfway between Sagres and Lagos, **Salema** is regarded as an up-and-coming resort of this stretch, with a lively sprinkling of bars and restaurants, a pleasant beach with fishing boats and a market.

Burgau, 3.2 km (2 miles) east, is small and sleepy. Fishing boats pulled up onto the end of the road leading down to the beach jostle with cars. The beach here is less attractive than those at neighbouring Luz or Salema, but the small village retains its easygoing character.

Luz is a pleasant seaside town. All that remains of old Luz is the church and, opposite, the **fortress**, which has been attractively renovated and converted into a restaurant. There is a good beach with watersports facilities and large, flat rocks where holiday-makers bask like lizards in the sun.

LAGOS

Lagos, the principal resort of the western Algarve, is the rare beach town that offers something for everyone. By night Lagos is lively, with outdoor restaurant terraces and bars attracting a hipper crowd than most resorts on the coast, and by day it combines a rich historical past with a busy present. Attractive beaches are just on the outskirts of town, so it is not a classic resort in the style of Praia da Rocha.

Your first view of Lagos will probably be from the long, riverside Avenida dos Descobrimentos, which divides the old walled city from the port. At the other end of the avenue, the well-restored fortress, **Forte da Ponte da Bandeira**, once guarded the entrance to the harbour in the 17th century. Cross the river to see busy fishermen, handsome boats anchored in the marina and the fine view of the city above the walls. Many of the streets rising towards the top of town are narrow, cobbled and more accustomed to donkeys than rental cars. Though Lagos town still retains a good part of its original walls – most of them from the 16th century, but part-Roman in places – they have been rebuilt and expanded over the centuries. Climb the ramparts for fine views over the port and out to sea.

Lagos was an important trading port under the Moors, but the town enjoyed its heyday after the Reconquest. It was

Reading the Map

Finding your way around the Algarve is easy, provided you master a few essential words. Here's a list of most of the words you're likely to come across during your explorations:

avenida	avenue	miradouro	belvedere
mosteiro	monastery	mercado	market
paço, palácio	palace	capela	chapel
parque	park	casa	house
ponte	bridge	castelo	castle
praça	square, plaza	cidade	town
praia	beach	claustro	cloister
rio	river	convento	convent
rua	street	saída	exit
entrada	entrance	sé	cathedral
torre	tower	fortaleza	fortress
largo	square	igreja matriz	parish church
Câmara Municipal	Town Hall	turismo	tourist office information

proclaimed the capital of the Algarve, and the governor's palace became the headquarters of Prince Henry. A formal statue of Henry, seated with sextant in hand, has been erected on a plaza (Praça Dom Henrique) next to the main avenue. Arguments persist over the exact whereabouts of the prince's School of Navigation, but it seems almost certain that Lagos was the principal shipyard and port serving his team of explorers.

> **Prior to 1991, the Sagres fortress lay in ruins from its destruction in 1587 by Sir Francis Drake.**

Those were glory years, but some of what was glorious in those heady times today seems reprehensible. Explorations along the west coast of Africa in the mid-15th century established a flourishing slave trade, and Lagos was a key player in human commerce. Just behind the statue of Henry, on the corner of Rua da Senhora da Graça, you can still see the small arcade where Portugal's first slave auctions took place. A small plaque states simply **Mercado de Escravos** (Slave Market). Most other historic buildings around the square succumbed to the devastating earthquake of 1755 *(see page 18)*. The majority of the city's attractive buildings thus date from the late 18th and 19th centuries.

☞ On Rua General Alberta da Silveira, the tiny chapel **Igreja de Santo António**, an exuberant gilt Baroque work and one of the Algarve's finest churches, was rebuilt soon after the earthquake. The church, a national monument dedicated to St Anthony, has a handsome display of 18th-century blue-and-white glazed tiles and a brightly painted wooden ceiling. In the floor you'll find the tomb of an Irish colonel, Hugh Beatty, a soldier of fortune who commanded the Lagos regiment of the Portuguese army in the late 18th century, and who must have been held in very high esteem to have been awarded such a prestigious final resting place.

The ornate ceiling in the chapel of Santo Antonio in Lagos is a highlight of one of Algarve's most beautiful churches.

The entrance to the church is actually through the curious and eclectic museum next door, **Museu Regional de Lagos**. Rooms display sacred art, archaeological remains, the original charter of Lagos, holy vestments and a bizarre collection of creatures, like a science experiment gone wrong: an eight-legged goat kid preserved in formaldehyde, a one-eyed sheep, a cat with two faces.

The main street of Lagos is the charming, cobbled **Rua 25 de Abril**, packed with restaurants, bars and antiques and ceramics shops. The side streets hold some good art (and craft) galleries and plenty of rewards for exploration. The square at the end of 25 de Abril holds a curious statue, which some liken to an extraterrestrial, of the boy-king Sebastião. In 1568 Sebastião became king of Portugal at age 14. A decade later he embarked on a disastrous voyage to

Morocco to fight the Moors. At least 7,000 troops died, the king included (though many refused to believe he had perished, and Elvis-like sightings were common).

The beaches near Lagos range from **Meia Praia**, 1.6 km (1 mile) to the east, a long (4 km/2½ mile) flat stretch, to pocket-sized coves just west of the city. Weird and wonderful rock formations, and steep cliffs that glow orange at sunset, have made them some of the most photographed in Europe; head for **Praia de Dona Ana** and **Praia do Camilo**, both small, pretty and crowded (street signs show the way to each).

At the southern tip, just before it turns west to Sagres, are the coast's most spectacular sights. **Ponta da Piedade** (Point of Piety) is the mother of all stack and cliff formations along the Algarve, a stunning terracotta family of bridges, terraces and grottoes. There is no beach here, but there are great views from above, and in season (spring to autumn) boat trips depart from the foot of the long stairways that have been cut deep into the sides of the cliff.

For a complete change of scene, take a drive northwest towards the hills and **Bensafrim**. Here you can enjoy the Algarve of yesteryear and rolling undeveloped countryside, where people still live off the land. The tilled soil, a startling ochre colour, makes a bright backdrop for orange and lemon

The attractive Rua 25 de Abril is Lagos' main street, welcoming all who enter.

groves. Turn off towards the **Barragem da Bravura**, a dam, and you'll be rewarded with a sight every bit as inspiring as its name. This water, more akin to the English Lake District than sunny southern Europe, is also of great practical use, irrigating crops, including rice, around Lagos. A new road connects with the old EN 125 route and will undoubtedly open up this relatively undeveloped area.

PORTIMÃO AND ENVIRONS

Portimão, second in size only to Faro in the Algarve, is the most workmanlike town on the coast. But nestled around it are some of the Algarve's finest beaches, and that has transformed the area into one of the coast's most popular resorts. Praia da Rocha and Praia Três Irmãos in particular are lined with hotels and beach-goers. Most holiday-makers stay along this stretch.

Portimão sits at the confluence of the River Adade and the sea, and most of its local colour is down by the port, a haven of fishing activity. The top fish-canning spot on the Algarve, Portimão is renowned for its restaurants specializing in *sardinhas grelhadas* (grilled sardines). Though the town was settled by the Romans, it was one of the Algarve towns most damaged from the earthquake of 1755, and as a consequence has few buildings or monuments of historical interest. **Largo 1° de Dezembro** is a 19th-century addition, a park with 10 splendid blue-and-white *azulejo* benches, each illustrating a pivotal event in the history of Portugal. The park's name alludes to the date, 1 December 1640, when Portugal's independence from Spain was restored *(see page 18)*.

Much of the town centre is pedestrian-only and filled with shops. The main square, at Rua do Comércio and Avenida São João de Deus, is where you'll find the large and austere **Colégio dos Jesuítas** (Jesuit College). The church, constructed at the end of the 17th century, is the largest on the Algarve.

The Igreja de Nossa Senhora de Conceição in Portimão
bridges the gap between gothic and colonial architecture.

Around the corner, along Rua Machado dos Santos, is the handsome **Igreja de Nossa Senhora da Conceição**, sitting atop a small hill and incline of steps. The yellow-and-white church, originally constructed in the 15th century, has a beautiful Gothic portico with carved capitals, but looks like a colonial church you might find in Brazil, due to its reconstruction and remodelling during the 18th and 19th centuries.

From the centre of town, head to the waterfront, especially if it's anywhere near time for lunch or dinner. You can almost follow your nose toward the heady aroma of grilled sardines. It will take you to the **dockside**, which is lined with simple restaurants, one after the other, all serving delicious, smoky sardines (and other freshly caught fish).

Choose whichever spot seems to be bustling with ravenous patrons. A plate of grilled sardines, prawns or squid and a bottle of house wine make a fantastic meal, and the prices are about as low as anywhere along the coast.

The hectic operations of the fishing industry used to take place here right under the noses of holiday-makers, with a frenetic 'bucket-brigade' hauling wicker baskets of fresh fish up from the boat holds to ice trays and waiting trucks, right next to dockside dining tables. The fishermen have now been pushed to a larger location on the other side of the river, but most sightseeing boats that tour the harbour and nearby grottoes include a quick trip to the new docks. You will still see fishing boats at anchor on the main quay, but the majority of river traffic here now is made up of private yachts, replica sailing ships on tourist excursions and tiny dinghies.

Fishy Business

At night out on the ocean, a mile or two beyond the beach, you may see tiny specks of light glinting below the stars. These are the lanterns of a small fleet of fishing boats in a wide formation, luring fish into an elaborate net. For centuries fishing has been big business in the Algarve, but the biggest boom began 100 years ago when the canning industry came to the region. To this day, thousands of tons of fish, mostly sardines, with tuna coming in a close second, are caught, tinned and exported annually.

Those who have tasted plump and juicy sardines fresh from the quay at Portimão or elsewhere in the Algarve – they're best in summer, when mature – can only feel a little sorry for those who have to take their pleasures many weeks later, from a tin. If you're in Portimão during August, check out the Sardine Festival.

Portimão's other claim to local fame is its status as a comprehensive regional shopping centre. There is certainly a good variety of shopping here, including many international names, as well as outlets selling traditional crafts or locally made items. A market is often set up in the square opposite the Colégio dos Jesuítas.

Just 3 km (2 miles) down river from Portimão is **Praia da Rocha**, which became a holiday village for wealthy Portuguese families back at the end of the 19th century. It was 'discovered' by the British in the 1930s, when this 'beach of rocks,' strewn with extravagantly shaped eroded stacks, provided an inspirational refuge for writers and intellectuals. The belle époque Hotel Bela Vista is a surviving monument from those days.

Today the long, 2-km (1.3-mile) golden **beach** is still the main attraction, but the once-small village fronting the beach has been swamped by a sea of hotels and tourist facilities. Vestiges of the village's former grandeur can still be traced along the front, where grand old buildings jostle uncomfortably with high-rise blocks. The sprawl has entirely blurred Praia da Rocha's separate identity from Portimão.

At the very eastern end of the resort, guarding the River Arade, is the **Fortaleza de Santa Catarina de Ribamar** (St Catherine's Fortress), built in 1621 to defend Silves and Portimão against the Moors. Little remains of the actual fortress, but its courtyard is now an agreeable terrace where you can enjoy a drink and watch the sardine fleet returning to port. Directly across from the fort is the splendid, beige-coloured **Fortaleza de Ferragudo**, which looks like a giant sandcastle; note that this is closed to the public.

The old fishing village of **Ferragudo** nearby is well worth a visit. Despite its proximity to a main tourist enclave, and two excellent beaches of its own, it has resisted blatant commercialization, remaining a traditional fishermen's settlement. The opposite end of Praia da Rocha's long stretch is known as **Praia do Vau**. The splendid rock formations and coves continue, but this end of the beach is quieter and less developed than the eastern end.

Just west, **Praia de Três Irmãos** is the slightly upscale beach cousin of Praia da Rocha. The eastern end of the beach is a beautiful cove, hemmed in by cliffs and ochre rocks. Beyond it, the beach stretches to **Alvor**, a classic Algarvian fishermen's village. Narrow cobbled streets plunge downhill to a quay and market where boats bob at anchor on a wide, marshy lagoon. A handful of *tascas* and bars rustle up barbecued sardines. At the top of the hill, on Rua da Igreja, is Igreja Matriz, a delightful 16th-century church, with a

The Praia de Três Irmãos in Portimão boasts one of Portugal's most charming stretches of coastline.

delicately carved Manueline portico, perhaps the finest on the Algarve, and excellent 18th-century *azulejos* in the chancel. A large white-sand beach is the main focus of a recreational area that includes a golf course and a casino.

Between Alvor and EN 125, the main coastal road, are the **Abicada ruins** of a Roman village that dates back to the 4th century.

North of Portimão, and extending across the western half of the province, is the Serra de Monchique, a mountain range that protects the coast from the hot plains farther north. The *serra* is a verdant landscape of cork, pine and chestnut trees and low-lying areas are covered in wildflowers.

Two spots in the serra popular with visitors are Monchique and Caldas de Monchique (two separate villages). The highest point is Fóia. The first stop on the scenic journey along route N 266 is the spa village of **Caldas de Monchique**, known since Roman times for its therapeutic waters. Its hey-

The Manueline Style

During the reign of Manuel I (1495–1521), artists were inspired as never before by the discovery of far-off lands and the romance of daring sea voyages. The style they evolved, called Manueline after their king, celebrated this brave new age of maritime travel. Motifs such as anchors, knotted ropes, sails, terrestrial globes, marine plants and animals became the signatures of this period's sculptors and architects. In the 16th century, the style fell out of favour and by 1540 Portugal had joined with the rest of Europe in building in the more sober Renaissance style.

The most famous example of Manueline art is considered to be Lisbon's Belém Tower, but you can also see exuberant stonework all over the Algarve. Look out for the church portals and windows at Silves (the Igreja da Misericórdia), Alvor, and particularly at Monchique.

day was the Edwardian era, and many of the elegant buildings (including a casino and a handicrafts market) still date from this period. An air of nostalgia has long presided over this sleepy hollow, but a recent renovation programme has revitalised and widened its tourist appeal. The newly renovated hotels, restaurants and other facilities augment the more traditional shops.

In the meantime, Caldas de Monchique is a good place for a picnic and a stroll in the woods. The local waters are bottled and for sale across the Algarve.

To the north of Caldas, the road starts to weave uphill quickly, rising some 300 m (1,000 ft) in 5 km

Monchique's Igreja Matriz is notable for its distinctive blend of architectural styles.

(3 miles) past terraced farmlands and forests of eucalyptus, oak and cork. **Monchique** is a small market town, known for its handicrafts and the famous Manueline portico of its 16th-century **Igreja Matriz**. The beautiful, unusual church has Romanesque arches, stone columns, blue-and-yellow *azulejos* (tiles) and a handsome wood ceiling. If you wander around the town, you'll probably see artisans crafting shoes and pounding out walking sticks in closet-sized workshops.

High above the town, the ruins of a 17th-century convent, **Nossa Senhora do Desterro**, loom like a ghostly grey eminence. Closed to the public, it has apparently been seized by squatters, who've done little towards its upkeep other than festoon it with 'Private–Family' and 'Family Dog' signs.

The road continues upwards, passing roadside souvenir and fruit vendors and a few well-placed *miradouro* restaurants. At the end of the line is **Fóia**, almost 915 m (3,000 ft) above sea level, affording one of the best views in southern Portugal. There is no settlement here, just a collection of craft and souvenir stalls, a bar, a restaurant and an obelisk marking the highest point on the Algarve. On a clear day you can see from the bay of Portimão to the Sagres peninsula and pick out the rocky outcrops of the Lagos beaches.

Although you may welcome a breeze after the heat of the coast, the wind blows pretty briskly at Fóia, so you'll need a jacket or sweater. Don't worry if you've forgotten to bring one; the best buys among the souvenirs here are chunky hand-knitted cardigans and pullovers.

SILVES

Back down the main road toward Portimão, a turn-off to **Silves** leads to the former Moorish capital of the Algarve. More than eight centuries ago, Silves (then known as Chelb) was a magnificent city with palaces, gardens, bazaars and a huge red castle on a hill. Granada had the Alhambra, the legendary palace of the Moors, but the Algarve also possessed a city straight out of *Arabian Nights*.

The golden age of Silves began in AD 711 with the Moslem invasion. With redoubtable fortifications and a population in the tens of thousands, it was one of the strongest outposts in 12th-century Arab Iberia. The Crusaders attacked and took the city in 1189, only to see it recovered by the Moors two years later. A half-decade later, the Christian Reconquest captured Silves for good. However, the loss of Arabic wealth and the silting up of the River Arade left Silves almost literally high and dry, and by the time the bishopric of the Algarve was transferred to Faro in 1577, the town's population had dwindled to 140.

Its riches were stolen long ago, the once-great river is a silted shadow of its former self, and Silves is now just a dusty backwater, but the glorious setting remains. Surmounted by its red fortress, the white town climbs the hillside from the river, its medieval bridge still intact. The old city inside the gates still evokes the layout of the Jewish quarter and *alme-dina* of the Moors.

Though a castle of sorts Silves has existed here since Phoenician times, the present **Castelo dos Mouros**, on the site of Roman or Visigothic foundations, took shape after the Reconquest, though it preserves distinctly Moorish lines. Oleander and jacaranda soften its bellicose nature, and there are fine views over the tiled roofs of the town and surrounding country-side. A long-destroyed 'Palace of Verandas' once existed within the castle; today you can see only a deep well (60 m/200 ft).

The Castelo dos Mouros in Silves reflects the Algarve's Moorish and Roman past.

Next to the castle is the impressive Gothic **Sé Velha** (Old Cathedral) of Silves, built by the liberating Crusaders, some of whom are buried within, in the 13th century. The remains of a Moorish mosque are hidden behind the altar. Opposite the Sé is the 16th-century **Igreja da Misericórdia**, with a classic Manueline-style side door.

Wander down to the main square, the Praça do Municipio. The imposing **Torreão da Porta da Cidade** (Turret of the City Gate) gives you a good idea of how seriously defense of the city was taken. This sturdy, warlike structure now houses the peaceful municipal library (open to the public). Close by, on Rua das Portas de Loulé, is a modern **Museu Municipal** (archaeology museum). Here you can see part of a large Arab water cistern and other local finds.

The hills around Silves form a prosperous farming region;

figs, oranges, lemons, grapefruit, clementines and pomegranates are all grown in abundance in mile after mile of orchards.

Just outside the city, on the road to São Bartolomeu de Messines (route N124), is an important 16th-century religious sculpture. Known as the **Cruz de Portugal** (Cross of Portugal), it depicts the crucifixion of Christ on one face and the descent from the cross

A fishing boat exemplifies the bravado of Carvoeiro's seafaring culture.

on the other. Some speculate that the cross was given to the city upon the transfer of João II's remains to Batalha. The small, weather-beaten 3-m (9-ft) statue, easily missed, is really only of interest to aficionados of religious art.

If you are travelling by car, continue to the **Barragem** (dam) **do Arade**. The water collected in this reservoir surrounded by pine hills provides irrigation for the area's profitable orchards. It's a refreshing spot, perfect for a picnic as well as sailing and windsurfing.

Lagoa, a sizeable town east of Portimão, is the province's wine capital. The acidic *vinhos da casa* served in most restaurants on the Algarve come from here. Lagoa wine, both red and white, is more powerful than ordinary wine, and the extra degree or two of alcoholic content can creep up on you. The local tourist office can arrange tours of wineries and tastings (Adega de Cooperativa de Lagoa; Tel. 282/342 181; 24 hours in advance). New golf courses are being built in the area, but there's little else to detain visitors.

From Lagoa, turn south about 5 km (3 miles) to the charming resort of **Carvoeiro**, an archetypal small Barlavento resort. The beach is about the size of a tablecloth compared with some of the expanses to the east. A single road runs down through a pretty valley until it comes to a small crescent of sand shared by families of sunbathers and fishing boats. Above, rows of bright white houses perch on red sandstone cliffs, while cafés and restaurants fill the spaces in between. The original village of Carvoeiro is now fairly commercialized, but to many people it remains one of the coast's most attractive resorts.

A narrow road follows the cliffs eastwards to the geological curiosity of **Algar Seco** ('dry gully'). Among other weird and wonderful shapes, wind and wave erosion have created a double-decker stone arch. There are walkways down to a lagoon

Porches is well known for the hand-painted pottery produced in local shops.

enclosed by menacing rocks, and if weather conditions are calm, this open-air grotto is a paradise for snorkellers.

Continue east and you will find three more beaches whose relative isolation has thus far protected them from development. They are (heading east) **Vale de Centianes**, **Praia do Carvalho** and **Praia de Benagil**. The last one in particular is superb, and is approached down a vertiginous road flanked by massive cliffs. Back inland, just off the main road, is the attractive little village of **Porches**, with some classic, white Algarvian houses and filigreed chimneys. Porches is famous throughout Portugal for its hand-painted pottery, though you won't find much in the village itself. The shops of greatest renown are along the EN 125 route. Olaria Algarve (Tel. 282/352 858), better known as Porches Pottery, is the biggest and best of these, with highly original designs and unique colours. Inside you can usually see a trio of women painting pieces. There's also an attractive little café-restaurant, itself decorated (of course) with wonderful ceramics. A little further east is Casa Algarve, which sells pottery and handicrafts in an attractive old house. More than others, it specializes in large-scale *azulejo* panels.

The coastal development nearby along the cliff tops continues apace. However, the vast majority of apartments and villas here are low-rise, and perhaps because the road system is not fully developed here, this part of the coast has largely escaped the attentions of mass tourism.

One of the most photographed beaches along this stretch is **Nossa Senhora da Rocha** (Our Lady of the Rock). The rock in question is a promontory, boldly jutting out into the sea, surmounted by a little white fishermen's church. On either side of the rock are two lovely half-moon coves, framed by cliffs.

The beach of **Armação de Pêra** is one of the longest in the Algarve – a flat, golden stretch to the east, picturesque rock stacks and small coves to the west. The massive development on the east end of town, though, has pretty much run roughshod over the natural beauty of the area, all but eclipsing the former fishing village. On the front, however, there is a pleasant esplanade and a small fortress, built in 1760 and home to a pretty chapel.

ALBUFEIRA

Albufeira, at one time a picturesque fishermen's town, has grown wildly in recent years to become the leading resort in the Algarve. The area now generally referred to as Albufeira encompasses the coast from beyond Galé in the west all the way to Praia da Falésia, just before a marginally distinct resort area begins at Vilamoura. Parts of the commercial sprawl, while rarely grotesque, still overwhelm the little town at their centre.

Once you're off the traffic-squeezed main arteries, you'll find that Albufeira's old town preserves a surprising bit of traditional charm. The cluster of whitewashed buildings includes a number of Moorish arches and three small churches.

Its magnificent setting – enormous, pockmarked sandstone cliffs rise above a huge beach lined with colourful fishing boats and hundreds of sunbathers – has proved resistant to development ruin. The gently sloping sands are perfect for family holidays, and if you are looking for a little more privacy you can escape the crowds by heading farther east along the sandy coast. A tunnel links the centre of the town with the main beach.

When tractors haul the fishing fleet ashore, sunbathers jump from their towels to gape at the catch – 1-metre (3-foot) eels, still flapping; foot-long, spiny lobsters still snapping; and bucketloads of flat and silver fish. The famous beachside fish market buckled under logistics problems years ago and moved just north of the centre. It is still worth a visit, however, and you will also find fruit, vegetables and flowers on sale.

Albufeira's name evokes its Moorish roots. Indeed, the North African occupiers called it Al-Buhera ('castle on the sea'). Its cliff-top position and labyrinthine street plan provided an easily defensible spot for the Moors, and Albufeira proved one of the last towns to fall during the Reconquest. Its layout, however, did not save it from the 1755 earthquake, during which the town was almost completely destroyed.

Modern Albufeira has fallen prey to mass tourism – international bars, cafés and nightspots pump out loud music day and night. There is little traditionally Portuguese

Visitors entering the Praia da Falésia in Albufeira are dwarfed by its high cliffs.

about its raucous central square, but there are quiet spots to be found. And what brings all the tourists here, the Atlantic, is just a splash away. From almost any vantage point, the view of old Albufeira sloping up a gentle hill and its seascape is incredibly spectacular.

With so much activity to the east, the excellent beaches west of town are relatively uncrowded. The best are **São Rafael**, a beautiful, sandy strip with some splendidly shaped rocky outcrops, and **Coelha**, **Castelo** and **Galé**, three small, beautiful coves.

One of the most picturesque towns in the province is the lovely village of **Alte**, about 30 km (18 miles) north of Albufeira. It is entered in romantic fashion, across a small, white bridge over a babbling stream that runs through town and waters a valley thick with oranges, pomegranates and figs.

The architectural highlight of the village is the 16th-century Igreja Matriz, entered through a classic Manueline portal. The church keeper will enthusiastically point out the many elaborate chapels and the rare 16th-century Sevillana *azulejos.* The rest of Alte is the Algarve of postcards – white-washed houses along narrow streets, colourful windows, filigreed chimney pots and red-tiled roofs. And while their character may at first seem uniform, you won't see two houses the same.

Follow the stream upriver and you come to the popular Pequena Fonte (Little Fountain) springs, where a restaurant and occasional folk dancing draw visitors. The setting is delightful and a perfect spot for a picnic.

If you continue east on N-124, you'll pass rolling hills and come to the pretty village of **Salir**, which is built on the edge of a steeply rising ridge and has two fine lookout points. The first is in the village itself, alongside the 16th-century parish church and water tower (don't miss the delightful gardens next

door). The other, with the best views, is the adjacent peak, which once held a Moorish stronghold (follow signs to the Castelo). All that remains of the castle are the bases of four huge turrets (12th–13th century) and some excavations. The old castle grounds are home to a tiny hamlet, complete with its own church. The panoramic views across to the main part of Salir and the surrounding countryside are spectacular, and there is even a tiny *miradouro* (belvedere) café here.

EAST FROM ALBUFEIRA

An elderly woman walks through the Arab fortress in the town of Salir.

Loosely grouped with Albufeira are beaches to the east. Here, the coastline features the last of the dramatic rock formations that have made the Algarve so famous. At appealing **Olhos d'Agua**, a single road leads between pine-covered cliffs down to a soft, sandy beach shared by a gaily painted fishing fleet, eroded sandstone formations and sunbathers. The resort derives its name from the 'eyes of water' that flow from strangely formed rocks, visible only at low tide.

Falésia is a beautiful beach framed by high cliffs, but to reach it you need to negotiate the grounds of the Sheraton

Algarve, whose elevator down to the beach is for guests only. There are other excellent beaches at **Santa Eulalia** (longer and more open than Olhos de Agua), **Balaia**, **Praia da Oura** and **São João**. The latter two are regarded as satellites of Albufeira and may well be where you are staying on a package holiday to Albufeira. The

> Is this the right direction to …
> *Vou bem para …?*

centre of activity along this beach hinterland is the infamous 'strip' – a long street leading up to the hilltop area known as Montechoro. As the name indicates, it's lined with a motley collection of bars, restaurants and nightspots.

Nearby **Vilamoura** is a wholly planned and sanitized community – Europe's largest 'from-scratch' private tourist undertaking. From high-rise hotels and sprawling villas that line manicured golf courses to the 19th-hole club bar and the Algarve's biggest marina, it is undeniably well done, but it could be anywhere. Still, it's a major draw for those who have their clubs ready for a golfing holiday; several of the Algarve's best courses have been sculpted out of the area.

As new as everything looks and feels, the marina designers were not the first to take advantage of Vilamoura's harbour. The Romans built a dock in the same place and established an important fishing centre here. The Roman remains of **Cerro da Vila** were unearthed across the road from the marina. Aside from some low-level excavations showing the elaborate water-piping system and surviving mosaics and ceramics, there is also a small museum displaying everything from fishhooks to lamps, appealing to any student of archaeology.

A little further west, **Quarteira**, once a quiet fishing village, is today virtually unrecognizable, subsumed under an onslaught of rows and rows of apartment buildings. The busy resort has a long, golden beach, and there are good,

The Ria Formosa Nature Preserve in Quinta do Lago combines natural beauty with a first-rate golf course.

cheap restaurants in the old quarter where locals and adventurous visitors mingle. The municipal market still stands on the beach; every Wednesday one of the largest and busiest markets on the Algarve – offering fish and produce – is held next to it.

East of Vilamoura and Quarteira, the Algarvian terrain begins to change. The rugged, rocky lines of the Barlavento coast west of Faro give way to the long, flat beaches of the east.

The small crossroads town of **Almancil** has shops, cafés and businesses, many of which are dedicated to serving English expatriates. But the town, of modest interest itself, is best known for what lies in its vicinity. Many of these expats live just a few miles south on the coast, and it is here that two of the Algarve's most luxurious and exclusive resorts are found. Surprisingly, given their status, neither

Vale do Lobo nor Quinta do Lago are well sign-posted off
the main road.

Each is reached down long roads that become
progressively more private-looking as the beach nears. **Vale
do Lobo** means 'Valley of the Wolf', but it could just as
well mean 'Valley of the Dolls'; it is a security-conscious,
maze-like villa community concealed behind a giant
entrance gate. Guards do their best to keep the beach the
domain of the expatriate and wealthy tourist classes.
Quinta do Lago, a few miles down the coast, refers to the
hotel of the same name, once owned by Prince Faisal of
Saudi Arabia, and the luxury homes that have sprouted up
around it. Quinta do Lago has one of the finest golf courses
on the Algarve, which is designed delicately along the **Ria
Formosa Nature Preserve**. The beach is reached across a
long, nostalgic wooden bridge that crosses wetlands and
bird sanctuaries. On the beach is a terrific, if expensive,
restaurant for fresh-caught fish, which you pick out and
have grilled.

Back toward Almancil is one of the Algarve's top
attractions, but if you're not looking closely, it's easy to
miss. About 16 km (10 miles) west of Faro, a simple white
church stands out on a small hill overlooking the
thundering highway. A sign simply says 'S. Lourenço' –
indicating the turn-off to **São Lourenço do Mato** (Church
of St Lawrence of the Woods). Inside is one of the most
extraordinary displays of *azulejo* design you'll ever see.
Every square inch of the Baroque, 15th-century church –
its walls, vaulted ceiling and cupola – is covered with
hand-painted, blue-and-white ceramic tiles. Most date from
the early 18th century and depict biblical scenes detailing
the life of St. Lawrence, born across the border in Huesca,
Spain. The only element of the church not blue-and-white

is the carved, gilded altar. The ensemble is a stunning sight, not to be missed.

Loulé, north of Almancil, is a regional produce centre with a large Saturday market, known for its leather, lace and copper goods. Loulé is a prosperous town with an ambitious, modern boulevard complete with outdoor cafés that are jam-packed on market day. Coach parties come from far and wide to shop at the colourful, bustling market.

> *Azulejos* (ah-zoo-*lay*-zhoos) are hand-painted, glazed ceramic tiles introduced by the Moors. The name is probably derived from *al-zuleiq*, Arabic for small polished stone.

There are actually two markets. Fresh produce, including fish, is sold in a mock-Moorish hall, while a 'gypsy market' is held towards the opposite end of the boulevard. Just below the permanent market halls, on the main Praça da República, you'll find a well-preserved section of the medieval castle walls (which were much damaged by the 1755 earthquake). The ramparts afford excellent views from the town, and set into the castle remains is a modest local museum. Also worth visiting are the **Igreja Matriz** (São Clemente), a 13th-century Gothic church with 18th-century *azulejo* tiles; the **Convento da Graça**, with a terrific Manueline portal; and **Ermida de Nossa Senhora da Conceição**, a small church prized for its Baroque altar and ceramic tiles.

In the streets directly below the castle walls, you may well hear the sounds of craftsmen beating copper – from whom you can buy direct. You can also see artisans at work on the pottery wheel, producing leather goods (such as decorated saddles and bridles) and furniture. The craftsmen of Loulé are said to be the descendants of a community of Muslims who found refuge in the district at the end of the Reconquest. If you are in the Algarve in springtime, don't miss the Loulé

Carnival. The parades, 'Battle of Flowers' and musical celebrations are the best of their kind in the region.

The flower-lined road from **Loulé** to **São Brás de Alportel**, another market town and site of one of only two government *pousadas* (inns) along the Algarve, passes through rolling orchards of fig, olive and orange trees. It's best to visit the town on Saturday, when the lively market transforms its otherwise sleepy character. You may wish to pay a visit to the lovely **Museu Regional do Algarve** (Ethnographic Museum), where exhibits of Algarvian costumes are well staged in a large, old house 90 m (100 yards) or so off the main square.

In this northern part of the southern province, life is visibly slower and more rustic; bonneted ladies in black walk along the roadside, old men bounce up and down on donkeys, and families pluck almonds from the trees with long sticks.

On the road toward Faro is a pair of historical sights. The **Palácio de Estói** (currently closed to the public) is a most curious find. The charming Rococo palace, found through a small side gate just to the left of the church steps in the town centre, once belonged to the Dukes of Estói. Begun during the mid-18th

The Palácio de Estói is a fascinating, forgotten place in the countryside.

century, in palatial terms, it's rather small, abandoned and visibly dilapidated; however, it is soon to be transformed into a new *pousada* (a state-owned hotel, usually – as here – housed within an historic building) and should be one of the most interesting *pousadas* in which visitors can stay. Even prior to the conversion, it is a spectacular sight.

> **Speed Limits**
> Highways: 120 km/hr (75 mph)
> Main roads, rural areas: 90 km/hr (55 mph)
> Urban areas: 50 km/hr (30 mph)

Its faded glory includes balustrade terraces and staircases with splendid bursts of bougainvillea, busts of historic characters impaled on the parapets, brightly coloured wall tiles and formal gardens.

The dusty **Villa Romana de Milreu** (Roman ruins of Milreu) is located 1.5km (1 mile) down the road from the village, on the route towards Faro (a small sign on the side of the road reads 'Ruinas de Milreu'). Some 1,400 years before the Palace of Estói was erected, Milreu was also the large country house of an eminent person. The knee-high walls that trace the outline of this once-luxurious establishment are still clearly visible. The tall, semi-circular tower ruin is thought to have been a temple to pagan water gods at one time; however, by the fifth century it had clearly been converted to a church.

FARO

Faro, the provincial capital of the Algarve, is also the one that seems to get the least respect from tourists. Many fly into Faro, beeline directly to their resorts and return two weeks later, bypassing the city for the airport. Those who take the time – a day is sufficient – to explore Faro find an atmosphere quite distinct from the resort-heavy coast. Faro has a greater wealth of cultural and historic monuments than any other

Algarvian town, a picturesque old quarter and best of all, tourists never overrun authentic Portuguese restaurants, cafés and bars.

Faro was, always an important town, even during Roman times, when it was allowed to coin its own money. It continued to thrive under the Arabs; its name may be derived from the name *Harune,* one of the old city's ruling families. The Christians recaptured Faro in 1249, completing the Reconquest, and the city prospered, becoming the Episcopal see of the Bishop of the Algarve in 1577. But in 1596, when it was Spanish territory, an English fleet commanded by Queen Elizabeth I's favourite, the Earl of Essex, sacked and burned the capital.

Until comparatively recently, when the area silted into a tidal flat, Faro was a commercial and fishing port open to the Atlantic. Indeed, the Earl of Essex's fleet had sailed right up to the city's Arab fortifications. Today small fishing boats and pleasure craft must zigzag carefully amid the dunes and then creep beneath the railway bridge to enter the sleepy harbour.

Filigreed Flues

Tourism has often been called an industry without chimneys, but not so in the Algarve, where smokestacks – albeit graceful, lattice creations, reminiscent of Moorish lanterns – have become a trademark of the region. For hundreds of years, Algarve homeowners have taken great pride in the beauty and originality of their chimneys. The popular dictum is the more elaborate the chimney pot, the wealthier the owner. Originally carved of wood, later ceramic, and then eventually concrete was used. The area around Faro and Olhão in particular enjoy a strong reputation for rooftop art, but keep your eyes skyward and you'll see pretty chimney pots all over the Algarve.

The main entrance to the circular old town, near the harbour, is the 19th-century **Arco da Vila**, a lovely arch and bell tower habitually crowned by a venerable family of nesting storks. Beyond the arch, a cobbled street, worn slick by centuries of tramping feet, leads up to the splendid expanse of the **Largo da Sé** (Cathedral Square), best seen in the evening when floodlit and free of cars.

The **Sé**'s unusual cathedral tower, main portico and two interior chapels are all that remain of the original 13th-century Gothic building. The entrance is at the side – as you enter, look out for the remains of the *capela dos ossos* (Bone Chapel). Inside are some fine examples of *azulejos* and superb statues and carvings, one of the Algarve's top collections of 17th- and 18th-century sacred art. Climb the tower for fine views over the whole of Faro.

Across the square is the **Paço Episcopal** (Bishop's Palace), an excellent example of the plain *chã* style prevalent during the 17th century. To its right is the *Câmara Municipal* (Town Hall).

The **Convento de Nossa Senhora da Assunção** (Convent of Our Lady of the Assumption), which contains the most beautiful cloister in

The Arco da Vila lies at the entrance to Faro, one of Algarve's overlooked gems.

southern Portugal. The first Renaissance building in the Algarve, it was constructed in the 16th century on the site of the old Jewish quarter (Faro had a sizeable Jewish population in the Middle Ages). Abandoned as a convent in the 19th century and then put to use as a cork factory, it has now been beautifully restored as a museum devoted to archaeology, the **Museu Arqueológico Infante Dom Henrique**. The principal exhibit is a 2,000-year-old Roman floor mosaic measuring 9 m (30 ft) long and 3 m (10 ft) wide. Unearthed in Faro, it is nicknamed the 'Ocean Mosaic', for it depicts a bearded sea-god (though the bulldozer that discovered it in 1976 shaved off the lower half of his face). There are also busts taken from the Roman ruins at Milreu. Displays of Portuguese art are housed in the many rooms off the cloister.

Nearby is the **Ermida de Nossa Senhora do Repouso** (Hermitage of Our Lady of Rest), a tiny 18th-century chapel carved out of the ancient Moorish arches.

The real attraction of Faro's old town, however, is not its set-piece buildings, but the quiet, hidden, timeless flavour of its tiny houses and narrow, cobbled alleyways. A good place to sit and absorb some of it is the friendly Café do Largo, where classical music accompanies your coffee.

Just outside the old quarter is the **Igreja de São Francisco** (Church of the Third Order of St Francis), begun in the late 17th century. Narrative tiles adorn the main chapel and vaulted ceiling, which displays a terrific panel of the Coronation of the Virgin Mary.

In the centre of town, across from the harbour, the cobbled and shaded municipal **Jardim Manuel Bívar**, created in the 15th century as the Queen's Square, is a popular meeting place for young and old alike. In its centre are an open-air café and an old-fashioned bandstand. Several handsome 16th- to 18th-century mansions surround the square, including the Banco de Portugal building and the Palácio Belmarço.

As in several other Algarve towns, the main shopping area of central Faro is pedestrian-only, and cafés and restaurants spill out onto the street, fish displays and all. Rua de Santo António is the main thoroughfare. At its far end is the **Museu Regional do Algarve** (Ethnographic Museum), with displays of local handicrafts, reconstructions of rooms in a typical Algarvian house, and a colourful water-cart that Manuel Ignacio Miguel of Olhão operated for 60 years, almost up to his death in 1974. The museum sits on the edge of Faro's Mouraria, or old Moorish quarter. It's worth wandering the streets that lead to **Largo do Pé da Cruz** and the attractive little 17th-century chapel of the same name (Our Lady of the Foot of the Cross).

The new town, an expansion dating from the 19th century, is west of here. Two churches, which face each other across a large and congested plaza, are worth seeing. The **Igreja de São Pedro** (Church of St. Peter) is the smaller of the two, built in the 16th century. It has a carved Baroque retable and a couple of Rococo chapels.

But Faro's finest church is **Igreja do Carmo** (Carmelite Church), which took most of the 18th century to build. The promise of its twin belltowers and stately façade is matched by a beautiful gilded interior, but the greatest attraction is the macabre **Capela dos Ossos** (Chapel of Bones). This 19th-century curiosity, like a similar chapel in the town of Évora farther north, is constructed of the skulls and bones of monks, unearthed from the friars' cemetery. Depending on your tolerance for such things, it is either fascinating or sick beyond belief.

Less ghastly is the **Jewish Cemetery**, on the outskirts of town (off Rua Leão Penedo, near Praça dos Bomberos de Faro). Dating to the early 19th century, it has more than one hundred tombstones in Hebrew, testimony to the once-important Jewish community in Faro.

The Capela dos Ossos, with walls made from human bones, never fails to intrigue.

Few people seem to do it, but it is well worth spending a night or two in Faro, especially if you've already spent some time in a traditional Algarvian beach resort. Watch the sun setting over the fishing boats in the lagoon while you have a drink in the splendidly old-fashioned, cavernous Café Aliança, the city's oldest café. Faro also has some lively music bars.

Faro's beach, the **Praia de Faro**, is noted for its watersports. You can drive there across the single-lane causeway linking the long, strip of dunes with the mainland (no buses or motor homes allowed), or in the summer catch a ferry from the pier by the old town. If the ocean is rough, simply cross to the opposite side of the sand spit and swim in the calm, warmer waters of the lagoon (though be aware, it can sometimes be muddy and a little unpleasant).

THE SOTAVENTO COAST

Heading east from the provincial capital of Faro, the first settlement of any size you will come to is the colourful fishing town of **Olhão**. A working port, it has made few concessions to tourism and is full of character.

Olhão has often been described as the 'little white Cubist town of the Algarve', its architecture likened to that of North African towns. That may have been the case some years ago, but modern development has strongly interfered with its once-distinctive

Pedro Alvares Cabral descobre o Brazil
24 de Abril de 1500

Colourful azulejos are often decorated with scenes from Portuguese history.

appearance. You can judge for yourself by ascending the bell tower of the parish church (**Nossa Senhora do Rosário**), which you'll find by winding your way through the narrow streets back to the Praça da Restauração (you may have to ask for access to the tower in the sacristy). Founded by King Dom Pedro II in 1698, the church has an impressive, scroll-decorated Baroque façade, brilliant white dome, stone belltower and a chapel at the rear, **Nossa Senhora dos Aflitos** (Our Lady of the Afflicted), where women often pray when their fishermen husbands are away at sea.

Instead of the red-tiled roofs and filigreed chimneys seen elsewhere in the Algarve, the Olhão skyline comprises flat-topped roofs of terraces called *açoeitas*. Look hard and you can still see the narrow, outside staircases leading to white-washed towers, where fishermen's wives, or perhaps smugglers, would look out for the incoming fleet.

The name of the square, **Praça da Restauração** ('Restoration Square'), recalls Olhão's most glorious moment, when an improvised local army rebelled against Napoleon's occupying forces in 1808. This insurrectionary zeal subsequently spread throughout the rest of Portugal and resulted in Olhão being awarded the title 'Noble Town of the Restoration.'

Olhão's fishing port is worth a look. The fishermen of the town have a reputation for hardiness – some used to earn a living in cod waters as far off as Newfoundland. During the past two centuries, however, some of the sailors have turned away from fishing and instead, taken to the cargo trade between Portugal and North Africa. This relatively recent link with the neighbouring continent may have been the inspiration for the local North African style of architecture. In any case, it developed long after the Moors had left the Algarve.

You're unlikely to see a boat coming in from another continent, but you are guaranteed the hustle, bustle, sights, smells and sounds of one of the **Olhão fish market**, one of the Algarve's best (the town is especially famous for its mussels and other shellfish). Adjacent to the voluminous market buildings are small, well-tended parks, one of which boasts several splendid benches decorated with blue-and-white *azulejos*. Just beyond the park on the other side, ferryboats depart regularly in summer for the barrier-island beaches of **Armona** and **Culatra** just offshore. These lovely, under-developed beaches are the jewels of the coastline between Faro and Tavira.

A little further along the coast, at **Fuzeta**, is another popular beach. There is some holiday development here, but as yet only on a small scale. Fuseta itself is little more than a creek of gaily-painted boats bobbing at anchor, while in the background local workers rake salt crystals into small white mountains punctuating the saline delta.

Turn inland, because the small village of **Moncarapacho**, with a fine old church, a sleepy village square and a local museum, is well worth the 8-km (5-mile) detour. The countryside around here is full of orange and almond groves and, as you head east (back on the main road) towards Tavira, olive groves and vineyards also start to appear. Tavira's grapes produce a good, rustic wine consumed all over the Algarve.

EAST TOWARD SPAIN

After the salty flavour of Olhão and the rural serenity of Moncarapacho, the aristocratic bearings of **Tavira**, one of the true gems of the Algarve, may come as something of a surprise. One of the region's most historic cities, its Moorish, Reconquista and Renaissance roots are clearly visible.

In the 1500s, Tavira had the largest population on the Algarve. This tuna-fishing port and self-assured town of historic churches, imposing classical-style mansions and riverfront gardens probably dates back as far as the Phoenicians or the Carthaginians. In fact, its seven-arched stone bridge of Roman origin is still in use.

Tavira's **castle**, in the middle of the *centro histórico* (old quarter), was a defensive structure built by the Moors. Climb the walls for a superb panoramic view of the city, but be careful, as the ramparts have no hand-rails. Within the walls is an attractive, fragrant garden.

The walls look directly onto the **Igreja de Santa Maria do Castelo** (Church of St Mary of the Castle), most likely built on the site of the old mosque. The Gothic portal is the only original 13th-century part of the building to have survived the devastating 1755 earthquake. In the chancel is the large tomb of Dom Paio Peres Correia, who drove the Moors out of Tavira in 1242.

Across the square, the ochre-coloured former convent, **Convento da Graça**, is being converted into a *pousada* by the Portuguese government.

Just down the hill, off Rua Galeria near the river, is the beautiful 16th-century **Igreja da Misericórdia** (Church of Mercy), a spectacular Renaissance edifice. The carved portico is especially fine, with a statue of Our Lady of Mercy under a canopy. The 18th-century interior contains excellent specimens of carved retables and tiles. There are at least two dozen other churches in Tavira; also worth a visit – though you may find them closed, – are the 13th-century **Igreja de Santiago** (St James Church), near the castle walls, and the 17th-century **Igreja de Sao Paulo** (Church of St Paul), across the river on Praça Dr Padinha. The church, part of a former monastery, has a unique feature: the floor of the transept is paved with bricks and stones painted with Spanish figures.

Rua da Liberdade, Tavira's main street, is lined with stately 16th-century mansions. A walk down any of the city's old streets will reveal handsome details of noble houses, such as double windows and latticed doors. A lively fruit and vegetable market is held by the banks of the River Gilão, and it is well worth crossing the Roman bridge to view more of the town's elegant houses and pretty flower-filled squares. Many of those houses have sloping triangular roofs, called *tesouros* (treasures).

A nice excursion from Tavira is to the nearby island **Ilha de Tavira**, where there is a huge and thoroughly appealing beach backed by sand dunes. Jetties leave from a point, Quatro Águas, a couple of kilometres (one mile) east of town.

Back on the mainland, a turn-off off the main road

From Tavira's castle walls, one can see the Igreja de Santa Maria do Castelo.

Stately grace emanates from every inch of Praça de Marquês do Pombal, the town square of Vila Real.

east (EN-125, still!) of Tavira leads a small number of visitors to a perfectly enchanting little whitewashed village overlooking the sea. Pretty **Cacela Velha** can't have more than 100 inhabitants. It has an 18th-century church, a telephone booth, a cemetery, an old well and a handful of well-tended, blue-and-white houses festooned with flowers. Below the town, along a spit of sand that's part of the Ria (estuary), are a few moored fishing boats.

East of here lies the fledgling resort of **Manta Rota**, a former fishing village and the high-rise canyons of **Monte Gordo**. The reason behind all this development is a long sandy beach, which stretches undisturbed for some 10 km (6 miles) between the two resorts and is backed by pine trees and dunes. Although the last in a long line of Algarve beach resorts (or the first, if you're coming from Spain) is not, by a long shot, the coast's most attractive, the beach and watersports facilities at Monte Gordo are enough to attract and entertain many serious sun-seekers. By night the casino is the focus of attention.

The Guadiana River, which runs into the Atlantic 3 km (2 miles) east of Monte Gordo, served as a natural frontier for 2,000 years, forming the boundary between the Roman provinces of Lusitania (Portugal) and Baetica (southern Spain). This explains the strategic importance of **Castro Marim**, a former fortress town rising from the flatlands to command the broad river. For five centuries its primitive castle-fortress was occupied by the Moors. After the Reconquest it became the home of the new Military Order of Christ (succeeding the disbanded Knights Templars). Look for the inscription inside the main entrance proclaiming that Prince Henry the Navigator, who was a governor of the order, once lived here. These days the castle itself is in need of defense and restoration, and although it may no longer be of any military value, its broad, unpolluted marshlands do attract large numbers of wading birds. The area is protected by the National Parks service and is very popular with birdwatchers.

A little to the south, the town of **Vila Real de Santo António** (the Royal Town of St Anthony) is the last of the Algarve's beach towns before Spain. The city was designed to be as grand as its name suggests, in order to impress the Spanish on the other side of the river. The town plan was the inspiration of the Marquês of Pombal, King José I's favoured architect, and the town was built in just five months in 1774, aping the grid layout of Lisbon's Baixa (lower city).

The town square, **Praça do Marquês do Pombal**, is the work of the royal architect, and the tour de force of Vila Real. The pavement's black-and-white wedges of stone radiate from an obelisk in the centre of the square like rays from the sun. Distinguished three-story, late 18th-century houses line the square, and orange trees soften the edges, adding colour and scent. Visit the small **Manuel Cabanas Museum**, just off the square, to see a nice collection of woodcuts that ranges from rustic scenes to famous statesmen and composers.

Today Vila Real is sleepy but quietly dignified. A walk around the old quarter reveals a number of fine, brightly painted houses along pedestrian-only streets. Vila Real de Santo António's main appeal is as the ferry port to **Ayamonte** across the water in Spain. The trip takes just 20 minutes – less time than it would take to drive to and over the new bridge – and the white town of Ayamonte is a fine sight as you approach it from the river.

EXCURSION TO LISBON

Until the 19th century, the overland journey from the Algarve to Lisbon, Portugal's capital city, took a week or more. Now it's only a few hours by road or rail, and you can fly from Faro in just 40 minutes.

For years Lisbon has had a reputation as a relatively quiet, easy-going town, lacking the hustle and bustle of other major European cities. But while this is still true to a degree, the gap is closing and Lisbon is becoming altogether more European.

The centre of Lisbon is small, compact and easy to get around in just a couple of days. Moreover, it has two lovely old quarters that are as full of character as any place in Europe. If you have more than two days, it is well worth visiting the surrounding region. The Estoril coast, including Cascais and the beautiful hilltop town of Sintra are two of the most popular excursions.

Exploring Lisbon

The city is built on hills – by legend seven, in fact many more – but the great thing for the visitor is the splendid vantage points and lookouts that these provide. The best place to start your tour of Lisbon is from the Moors' old castle, the Castelo de São Jorge, the king of all vantage points. From here you can look out over the whole of the city and along the broad Rio Tejo (River Tagus), spanned by the longest suspension bridge in Europe.

The castle is set just above Lisbon's most famous *bairro* (district), the **Alfama**. Here you will discover a labyrinth of narrow, crooked streets, cobbled alleyways, decaying old houses, former palaces, fish stalls and bars totally unknown to tourists. Little has changed here in decades, if not centuries.

A fine view of the Castelo São Jorge Castle, which sits atop the historic Alfama district.

Another majestic view of the city is from the **Miradouro de Santa Luzia**, a park just down the hill from the castle. Nearby is the **Sé** (Cathedral), which has an ancient, cavernous interior – one of perhaps a dozen first-class churches in the city. Adjacent to the cathedral is the **Igreja de Santo António da Sé**, named for Lisbon's patron saint, St Anthony of Padua.

Just beyond the dense quarters of the Alfama, is **São Vicente de Fora** (St Vincent Beyond the Walls), an Italianate church and monastic cloister. The latter is the true highlight: its courtyards are lined with blue-and-white *azulejos*, and the views from the roof are among the best in the city.

Down toward the river is the **Museu Nacional do Azulejo (National Tile Museum)**, devoted entirely to the art of painted and glazed ceramic tiles, a national art form. About 12,000 *azulejos* are on show here, from 15th-century polychrome designs to 20th-century art deco. A prized possession is the *Lisbon Panorama*, a 36m- (118ft-) long tile composition of Lisbon's riverside as it looked before the 1755 earthquake.

Like Alfama, the **Bairro Alto** (upper city) is a hilly area full of evocative houses decorated with wrought-iron balconies usually occupied by birdcages and flowerpots. At night the district is loaded with exciting atmosphere and is famous for its *fado* clubs. It's a relatively harmless place by day, but you should be on your guard if visiting after dark.

Perched on the edge of the Bairro Alto is the **Igreja do Carmo**, a convent devastated in the earthquake of 1755 but deliberately preserved as an atmospheric ruin and potent reminder of its impact. Nearby, the sumptuous, 16th-century **Igreja de São Roque**, features a small museum of sacred art.

The convent used to be connected to the lower city by the landmark 30-metre (98-foot) **Elevador de Santa Justa**, a lift situated off the

View from Bairro Alto, known for its narrow streets and lively nighlife.

Rossio square in the Baixa; however, the walkway linking the lift and the upper city was destroyed in a fire that swept through Lisbon in 1988, and nowadays you can only go to the top of the Elevador (definitely worth the effort for the excellent views from the top). This 1902 Victorian marvel of iron and glass was built by Raul Mesnier, not, as popularly believed, by Gustave Eiffel. To reach the upmarket shopping area of **Chiado**, now totally rebuilt after the 1988 fire, you have to slowly meander up behind the Elevador.

The Baixa is Lisbon's principal business district. The main square is the **Praça Dom Pedro IV**, better known as **Rossio**. Look out for the railway station, **Estação do Rossio**, which looks like a Moorish palace with horseshoe arches, just west of the square. Two blocks north is another lively square, **Praça dos Restauradores**, which leads to the leafy main thoroughfare, Avenida da Liberdade. The city plunges steeply downhill to the River Tagus and its most imposing square, **Praça do Comércio**, lined on three sides by gracious arcaded buildings and a vast triumphal arch. The grand square, wholly wiped out by the great earthquake of 1755, has seen its share of watershed political events: King Carlos and his son were felled by assassin's bullets in the square in 1908, and one of the first uprisings of the Carnation Revolution of 1974 was staged in this place.

Moving west and down toward the river from Praça do Comércio is the elegant residential neighbourhood called Lapa. Its standout sight is the **Museu Nacional de Arte Antiga** (National Museum of Ancient Art), Portugal's largest museum. Among its pieces of international renown are *The Adoration of St Vincent,* a multi-panel work attributed to the 15th-century Portuguese master, Nuno Gonçalves; and *The Temptation of St Anthony*, a fantastic hallucination by Hieronymus Bosch, tempered with humour and executed with mad genius.

Some 6 km (4 miles) west of Praça do Comércio lies the riverside district of **Belém**. It was from here that the age of exploration (begun on the Algarve) reached its zenith between 1497 and 1499, when Vasco da Gama's voyage to India opened up a major new sea route. During the following century, Portugal enjoyed a golden age of trade, and King Manuel celebrated the discoverers with two magnificent monuments.

 The most famous is the diminutive but exquisitely formed Torre de Belém. By contrast the majestic **Mosteiro dos Jerónimos** is Lisbon's largest religious monument and a formidable example of Manueline architecture. The church and its double-decker cloister survived the 1755 earthquake; in addition to housing royal tombs it also holds the relics of national heroes Vasco da Gama and the poet Luis de Camões. The monastery houses an archaeology museum, and next door is the **Museu da Marinha** (Naval Museum). Back down the street toward Lisbon is the **Museu Nacional dos Coches** (National Coach Museum), housed in the former riding school of the Belém Royal Palace.

Also in Belém is the modern **Padrão dos Descobrimentos** (Monument to the Discoverers). This huge waterfront sculpture depicts Prince Henry the Navigator at the prow of a stylized caravel that juts into the Tagus. The figures behind represent noted explorers, map-makers and astronomers whom Prince Henry mobilized in order to launch Portuguese ships into the history books.

Opposite the Padrão is the stylish **Centro Cultural de Belém**, which puts on temporary exhibitions and concerts and is also home to Lisbon's Design Museum. The centre has a good restaurant and terrace cafe , with fine views over the river and the Padrão dos Descobrimentos.

Lisbon's newest attraction is the park designed for the World Expo '98, which did much to reinvigorate the

The Padráo dos Descobrimentos, built on the edge of the Tagus, pays tribute to the age of exploration.

industrial eastern section of the city. Continuing to draw visitors to the riverfront **Parque das Nações** (Nations Park) is its world-class aquarium, the **Oceanário de Lisboa**, perhaps the world's top aquarium. The park is easily accessible by Metro.

Estoril Coast

Excursions follow the coast west from Lisbon, as the riverfront evolves into a series of Atlantic Ocean beaches. The most famous is **Estoril**, a resort about 24 km (15 miles) from Lisbon. A haven for deposed European royalty in the first half of this century, it retains a jet-set image, with Victorian villas and modern mansions. The famous casino, located at the top of the gardens of the Parque do Estoril, combines a night-club, restaurants, bars, an exhibition hall and a cinema.

In contrast to Estoril's pretentions, **Cascais** is an agreeable combination of fishing port, residence for aristocrats and tourist resort. Overlooking the main swimming/ fishing beach, the 13th-century citadel is one of the few buildings to have survived the earthquake and tidal wave of 1755.

Queluz

An easy half-day outing is to Queluz, 14 km (8 miles) west of Lisbon on the way to Sintra *(see below)*, home to a pretty pink palace commissioned by Pedro III. The sumptuous summer home was built in the second half of the 18th century and thrived during the reign of Maria I (1777–1799). The interior is a model of only slightly tattered splendour, but the exquisite Palace Gardens are the pride of Queluz, with imaginative fountains and armies of statues. Part of the palace has been converted into a *pousada*.

Sintra

Finally, excursions turn inland to the delightful hill town of **Sintra**, now a UNESCO-protected site. Since the 14th century, Portuguese kings have made the **Paço da Vila**, the royal palace in the centre of town, their summer home.

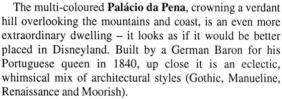 The multi-coloured **Palácio da Pena**, crowning a verdant hill overlooking the mountains and coast, is an even more extraordinary dwelling – it looks as if it would be better placed in Disneyland. Built by a German Baron for his Portuguese queen in 1840, up close it is an eclectic, whimsical mix of architectural styles (Gothic, Manueline, Renaissance and Moorish).

On a nearby hilltop, the ruins **Castelo dos Mouros** (Moors' Castle) date from the eighth and ninth centuries. Its conquest by the forces of Count Afonso Henriques in 1147 was considered a pivotal triumph in the Reconquest of Portugal.

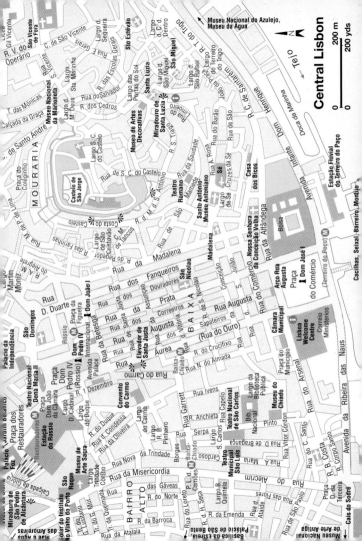

Central Lisbon

0   200 m
0   200 yds

N

→ Museu Nacional do Azulejo,
Museu da Água

Tejo

Cacilhas, Seixal, Barreiro, Montijo →

HIGHLIGHTS

Igreja de Santo António/Museu Regional de Lagos. Rua General Alberta da Silveira, Lagos. Tel. 282/76 23 01. Beautiful Baroque church and eclectic museum with sacred art and curiosities. Open Tues–Sun, 9:30am–12:30pm and 2pm–5pm. Admission fee.

Castelo dos Mouros. Silves; Tel. 282/44 56 24. Ruins of a deep red castle that crowns the ancient Moorish capital. Open daily, 9am–5pm (to 8pm in summer). Admission fee.

Igreja de São Lourenço do Matto. Off EN-125, Almancil. Tel: 289 39 54 51. Baroque, 15th-century church with every inch of the interior covered in blue-and-white ceramic tiles. Open Tues–Sat, 10am–1pm and 2:30pm–5pm; Mon, 2:30pm–5pm only. Admission fee.

Palácio de Estói. Rua da Barroca, Estói. Abandoned 18th-century Rococo palace and gardens that once belonged to the Dukes of Estói. Currently closed for conversion into a *pousada*.

Sé. Largo da Sé, Faro; Tel. 289/80 66 32. Cathedral with 13th-century Gothic foundations and tower miradouro. Open Mon–Fri, 10am–5:30pm, Sat 10am–1pm. Admission fee (museum and tower).

Museu Arqueológico Infante Dom Henrique. Praça Dom Afonso III, Faro; Tel. 289/82 20 42. Renaissance convent with beautiful cloister contains an archaeology museum with 2,000-year-old Roman floor mosaic. Open Mon–Fri, 9am–12pm and 2pm–5pm. Admission fee.

Igreja do Carmo/Capela dos Ossos. Largo do Carmo, Faro; Tel. 289/82 44 90. Carmelite Church with twin belltowers and beautiful gilded interior, with a macabre Chapel of Bones. Open Mon–Fri, 10am–1pm and 3pm–5pm; Sat, morning only. Admission fee.

Igreja de Santa Maria do Castelo (and castle). Alto de Santa Maria, Tavira. Church of St. Mary with a Gothic portal built within the walls of the old Moorish castle. Castle open, Mon–Fri, 9am–5pm; weekends and holidays, 10am–5pm.

LISBON AREA

Castelo de São Jorge (St. George Castle). Alfama. Old citadel of the Moors, with pleasant gardens within its walls and impressive views of the city from its ramparts. Open daily 9am–9pm; free. (See page 65)

Sé Patriarcal (Cathedral). Largo da Sé. Tel. 21/88 67 52. Fortress-like church begun in the 12th century and featuring fine tombs. Open Tues–Sat 9am–7pm; Mon–Sun 9am–5pm. Admission fee (to cloisters and museum). (See page 54)

Mosteiro dos Jerónimos. Praça do Império, Belém; Tel. 21/362 00 34. Belém's massive monastery, dating from the early 16th century, with impressive Manueline cloisters. Open Tue–Sun 10am–5pm. Church free; Admission fee for cloisters. (See page 68)

Museu Nacional de Arte Antiga (Museum of Ancient Art). Rua das Janelas Verdes. Tel. 21/391 28 00. Portugal's largest museum and collection of old masters, silver, gold, ceramics and oriental treasures. Open Wed–Sun, 10am–6pm; Tues, 2pm–6pm. Admission fee. (See page 67).

Museu Nacional do Azulejo/Convento da Madre de Deus. Rua da Madre de Deus, 4. Tel. 21/814 77 47. Collection of gorgeous 16th-18th- century painted ceramic tiles, occupying an old convent with a spectacular church. Open Wed–Sun, 10am–6pm; Tues, 2pm–6pm. Admission fee. (See page 66)

Oceanário de Lisboa. Parque das Nações. Tel. 21/891 70 02. Europe's largest aquarium, designed for Expo 98. Open daily, 10am–7pm. Admission fee. (See page 69)

Palácio Nacional da Pena. Estrada da Pena, Sintra.; Tel. 21/910 53 40. Fairytale palace built in 19th century by German baron for his wife, Queen Maria II. Open Tues–Sun, 10am–5pm (open until 6pm in summer). Admission fee. (See page 70)

Palácio Nacional de Queluz. Largo do Palácio, Queluz. Tel. 21/434 38 60. Rococo summer palace built by Pedro III for his mad wife, Queen Maria I. Opulent gardens. Open Wed–Mon 10am–5pm. Admission fee. (See page 70)

Palácio Nacional de Sintra. Largo Rainha D. Amélia, Sintra. Tel. 21/910 68 40. Royal palace with conical chimneys and Portugal's most important collection of 15th and 16th-century azulejos. Open Thurs–Tues, 10am–5pm. Admission fee (free Sun mornings).

WHAT TO DO

SHOPPING

What to Buy

Ceramics, Pottery and Azulejos. Portugal is renowned for its colourful, hand-painted and glazed pottery and tiles, and such items are generally much less expensive near the source than at home. You can buy a single blue-and-white tile (*azulejo*), an address plaque for your house, or a batch to assemble into a picture when you get home. Or purchase an entire set of plates. Some shops will paint tiles to order if you have a particular design in mind or they can copy a photograph. But remember that they can be heavy and fragile to carry home; inquire about shipping (there's even a 'Mail Boxes Etc.' franchise (on Praça da República; Tel.282/418 109) in Portimão, which ships for some of the pottery places in Porches, that will take care of the shipping for you).

Brass, Bronze and Copper. Candlesticks, pots and pans, old-fashioned scales, bowls, trays and even small stills for distilling your own gin can be found. *Cataplanas* (bronze pressure-cookers used to make the national dish) make delightful decorative or functional souvenirs.

Cork. Portugal is the world's leading producer of cork. You'll find place mats, intricate sculptures and other designs – and it's all as light as a feather.

Embroidery. Embroidered tablecloths, napkins and other items are found throughout the Algarve, especially at street markets, where they're likely to be literally thrust upon you. Haggling is absolutely acceptable at such places. Look also for the delicate hand needlework of the island of Madeira, items that are exceedingly well crafted but comparatively inexpensive.

Knitwear. Despite the generally warm weather along the Algarve, thick sweaters, caps and gloves, most of which come from the north of Portugal are some of the region's few genuine bargains. Stalls at the suitably windy venues of Fóia and Sagres are a surprisingly good value.

Leather. There was a time when leather goods were amazingly cheap in Portugal, but prices have risen considerably along with the tourist influx and 'Europeanization'. Still, you can find fashionable, relatively inexpensive shoes and handbags. Portimão is known for its selection of shops.

Many ceramics shops, selling hand-crafted items, are found on Rua 25 de Abril.

Wine. Portugal's wine industry produces not only excellent table wines from regions such as the Dão, Douro and Alentejo, but legendary port wine, which comes from the north. Vintages of port all the way back beyond your birth year can still be found in dusty bottles, but they are expensive.

Rugs. Attractive and excellently crafted hand-made rugs, mostly from the Alentejo region (north of the Algarve), are made as beautifully as they have been for centuries. The name to look for is Arraiolos, a type of colourful, rustic-looking wool rug named after a small town.

Wicker. Bags, mats, furniture, plant-holders, glass- and wine-holders, trays – you name it, you're likely to find it.

Where to Shop

Many shops on the Algarve stock pottery and leather items among the usual trinkets and souvenirs, but the most interesting spots for genuine handcrafts or local goods are regional markets. These colourful affairs are a mix of everyday wares for local consumption, genuine local handicrafts, leather goods and clothing. Usually held once or twice a month in the larger regional centres, they are popular with locals and tourists alike.

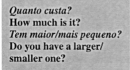

Quanto custa?
How much is it?
Tem maior/mais pequeno?
Do you have a larger/smaller one?

Another option is to go direct to the artisans' workshops. These are becoming increasingly difficult to find, as when the old craftsmen retire, their descendants are now turning to tourism instead of the traditional ways. Loulé and Monchique are probably your best bets.

Pottery and ceramics are found in and around every resort, but route EN-125 along the coast sells more ceramics and pottery than almost anywhere else in Portugal. The small town of Porches (pronounced like the German car) has a couple of the top shops in all Portugal: **Olaria Algarve** (Porches Pottery; Tel. 282/35 28 58), which has revived and updated long-forgotten Moorish styles, and **Casa Algarve** (Tel. 282/352 682). Other shops with good selections of hand-painted pottery include: **Casa Celiarte** (Rua 5 de Outubro, 39, Portimão) and **Amó** (Sítio do Tonel, Sagres; Tel. 282/62 47 48).

Good wine stores such as **Loja dos Vinhos** (Travessa dos Caldeireiros, Portimão; Tel. 282/41 68 71) exist in all of the big resorts.

ENTERTAINMENT

While Spain's southern coast is a magnet for ostentatious jet-setters who party all night, sophisticated nightlife has never really sprouted in the Algarve. Most evening entertainment is either hotel-based or set up specifically for tourists in bars and discos. But in quieter spots off the beaten tourist track and in less commercialised towns, you're more likely to find locals out for a drink.

Popular resorts such as Albufeira and Praia da Rocha throb to a disco beat, while visitors in smaller and newer resorts may have to rely on their hotel for entertainment. Lagos is one of the few resorts with a good selection of low-key bars and live-music venues. The 'Strip' in the modern section of Albufeira and the tourist village of Montechoro abound with all-night drinking and dancing opportunities – few of them classy – for sun-scorched tourists.

Casinos operate at Praia da Rocha, Vilamoura and Monte Gordo. They have restaurants with floor shows (open to families), while gambling takes place in a separate gaming room, from mid-afternoon to well into the following morning. You must be 21 or over to gamble and will need your passport or ID card. Dress is not formal but should be reasonably smart. Games include roulette, blackjack, baccarat and the Portuguese game of 'French bank'. The Casino in Praia da Rocha (Avenida Tomás Cabreira; Tel. 282/402 000), open daily until 4am, is particularly popular.

Another favourite attraction is the *fado* night, at which distinctive Portuguese folk music is performed. You'll find them at bars and hotels. The quality of performances is unlikely to rival the clubs in Lisbon's atmospheric *bairros*, but you can still get a taste for this quintessentially Portuguese musical expression. There are two kinds of *fado*: first, the melancholic,

Festivals and Folklore

In comparison to the flamboyant fiestas of neighbouring Spain, Portugal's festivals are low-key. But each and every town celebrates at least once a year on its saint's day, so check at the tourist information office when you arrive for forthcoming events (a monthly events leaflet and other publications with listings are available). The best of these is the *Carnaval* at **Loulé**, when spectacular flower-covered floats take to the street. Another lively spring festival is held in **Alte** on 1 May.

During May and June, the **Algarve Music Festival** schedules free classical concerts by local and international musicians, plus other performing arts, in some of the region's oldest churches. September brings the **National Folklore Festival** and in October there are two major fairs: **Feira de Outubro** at Monchique is famous for its market, while the **Feira de Santa Iria at Faro** is a lively traditional event lasting several days.

If you miss traditional dancing at any of these fairs, folklore shows are regularly staged in large resort hotels throughout the Algarve. Girls wear black felt hats over bright scarves, colourful blouses and aprons over skirts with hoops, and high-button shoes over white knitted stockings. The swift, whirling dances may also reveal traditional long underwear, worn in spite of the warm climate. Men are dressed more soberly, with trousers, waistcoats, cummerbunds and felt hats, mostly in black. Singers are accompanied by accordions, mouth organs and triangles.

There are basically two kinds of dances: the *corridinho*, or jig, whirlwind fast with stamping feet, and the *bailes de roda*, which are reels or square dances.

The Pequena Fonte restaurant in Alte hosts a lively folklore evening most nights. Look in local magazines for details of additional folklore events.

nostalgia-tinged variety, whose origins are unclear. It may have developed as a form of mourning for men lost at sea or it may be a relic of the days of slavery – a kind of Iberian blues. The other *fado* is much more upbeat, and, while lacking the emotional power of the former, at least gives the audience a chance to wring out their handkerchiefs. Typically a *fado* troupe consists of a woman dressed appropriately in black accompanied by a couple of men playing acoustic guitars.

Folk dancers in Albufeira keep the Portugal's unique fado tradition alive.

SPORTS

The Algarve is a top destination for sports holidays. With great weather and superbly designed courses, the region has long been famous for golf. Tennis is also big, and some former big names in British tennis have taken advantage of the favourable climate to set up schools here. And with around 160 km (100 miles) of south-facing beaches, there is plenty of scope for watersports enthusiasts.

Watersports. Most of the larger beaches have equipment for hire, but don't count on expert tuition everywhere. Aside from the main beach resorts, there are good facilities at Praia da Luz (where the Ocean Club has its own Watersports

Centre), the marina at Vilamoura, Quinta do Lago, Praia da Martinhal and Sagres.

Fishing. The waters of the Algarve provide some of the best big-game fishing in Europe. The Atlantic Ocean record, a blue marlin weighing more than 700 kg (1,500 lbs), was caught just 8 km (5 miles) off the coast of Faro in 1993. Shark (mostly blue, but occasionally copper, hammerhead, mako or tiger), marlin, billfish, large bass and giant conger are regularly hauled in. Swordfish and tuna can be caught further out. Sagres, Portimão and Vilamoura are the main centres, where you can board a boat or hire a crew. One outfit to consider is the **Big Game Fishing Centre** in Praia da Rocha (Urb. Portas da Rocha, Lote 7; 1; Tel. 282/425 866).

If the deep sea doesn't appeal, you can rent a small boat, rod and reel. The coast north of Sagres is one of the best spots to do this. You can also do like the locals and use a rod and reel off the rocks at a harbour entrance, or off the cliffs. Angling conditions are generally best in the winter, from October to mid-January.

Jet-skiing. For more high-speed fun on the water you can rent a jet-ski at Praia da Rocha, Quarteira, Alvor or Quinta do Lago, or hop aboard a 'water-banana' (a banana-shaped inflatable towed behind a speedboat) and skim the waves at Armação de Pêra and Praia da Oura.

Sailing. Dinghies and instruction are available at Praia de Luz, Quinta do Lago and Portimão. Sailing is also possible on the picturesque dam, Barragem do Arade. For bigger craft try the marina at Vilamoura or the Carvoeiro Club. Anchorage, as well as harbour facilities, are available at Lagos, Faro, Olhão, Portimão, Sagres and Vila Real. Boat cruises are available in nearly all spots along the Algarve, including neo-caravel cruises out of Portimão. **Bom Dia** offers Lagos-Sagres cruises, BBQ cruises, dolphin safaris and grotto trips departing from the Lagos marina (Tel. 282/764 670). **Mini Cruzeiros do Algarve** (Quay Q, Vilamoura Marina; Tel. 289 302 984), run a variety of coastal motor and sailing cruises.

Scuba-diving. Blue Ocean Divers in Porto de Mós offer reef, night, wreck, cave and freshwater dives from near Lagos. They also cater for complete beginners (Tel. 282 782 718). You can also explore the coastline with just a good snorkel and mask. Other centres include **Atlantic Diving** at Praia dos Aveiros and **Algarve-Sports** at Albufeira.

Spa. Not exactly a watersport per se, but the spa waters at Termas de Monchique (Caldas de Monchique) have drawn visitors since the 19th century. For more information on baths and fitness programmes, call Tel. 282/910 910.

Windsurfing. The most popular watersport along the Algarve coast – you'll find good instruction at Praia da Rocha, Ferragudo, Praia da Luz, Praia de Faro and Quinta do Lago. The last two have both sea and sheltered water, providing the luxury of calm conditions.

Land Sports

Golf. Although a year-round sport on the Algarve, the main season is from October to May. By the end of 2003 there will be 26 major golf courses (30 in all, a total of 513 holes) on the Algarve,

These colourful sailing vessels in Portimâo are just waiting to whisk you away.

many designed by the biggest names in the sport. Several are among the finest in Europe. All boast luxury clubhouses, manicured greens and immaculate fairways. The top courses are to be found clustered around Vilamoura and stretch west to Lagos. Look for the new Arnold Palmer designed Victoria golf course in Vilamoura, due to open in 2003. Green fees range from €50 to €200 (discounts possible) for 18 holes. All courses are open to visitors; many require an official handicap certificate and all require proper dress. The best (from west to east) are:

Parque da Floresta (Budens, near Salema): 18 holes. A spectacular rolling hillside course offering excellent value. Brand new 'Spa Floresta' opened in 1999. Tel. 282/690 000.

Palmares (near Lagos): 18 holes. A challenging course with an ocean panorama, plus high hills and deep valleys. Views of Bay of Lagos. Tel. 282/762 961.

Penina (near Portimão): 36 holes. The longest and oldest course, designed by Sir Henry Cotton, with a distinguished championship history (site of the Portugal Open). Waterways and lakes are a predominant feature. Championship course, required handicap 28 men/32 women. Tel. 282/420 200.

The Old Course (Vilamoura I): 18 holes. Designed by Frank Pennink, this is a classic English course, given a facelift in 1997. Golfers must present a certification of handicap no greater than 24 (men) or 28 (women). Tel. 289/310 341. For all Vilamoura courses, to reserve for more than two days ahead, ring central reservations. Tel. 289/310 333.

Pinhal (Vilamoura II): 18 holes. Originally designed by Frank Pennink and renovated by the famous American architect Robert Trent Jones in 1985. First 9 holes are among the pines, the last 9 have views of the sea. Tel. 289/310 390.

Laguna (Vilamoura III): 18 holes. Designed by Joseph Lee, opened in 1993. Known for its water hazards. Tel. 289/310 180.

At Sheraton Pine Cliffs, golfers may ponder the mysteries of the sea before concentrating on their next stroke.

Millennium (Vilamoura IV): 18 holes. The newest of the swanky courses at Vilamoura, designed by Martin Hawtree and opened in May 2000. Beautifully integrated into the environmental park at Vilamoura. Tel. 289/310 188.

Vale do Lobo: 36 holes. A rugged terrain with fine views, culminating in the 'most photographed hole in Europe' – a spectacular par-3 course stretching 192 m (210 yds) over two cliff ravines above the sea. Fairly narrow fairways. Tel. 289/393 939.

Vila Sol: 18 holes. Considered to have among the best fairways in the Algarve. Required handicap 27 men/35 women. Tel. 289/300 505.

Quinta do Lago: 36 holes. One of Europe's finest courses. American-designed with outstanding lush greens and roomy fairways – water is the biggest hazard. Tel. 289/390 700.

San Lorenzo (near Quinta do Lago): 18 holes. A new but already established course in a beautiful setting. Ranked by Golf World as the 5th-best course in Europe. Required handicap, 28 men/36 women. Tel. 289/396 522.

Sheraton Pine Cliffs (Praia Falésia): 9 holes. Although not the most challenging of the Algarve's courses, it's certainly one of the most picturesque, with a clifftop layout overlooking the sea. Tel. 289/500 100.

For details of facilities, write to the Portuguese National Tourist Board for a copy of their excellent golfing brochure, *Sportugal* or pick up a copy of *Algarve Golf Guide,* with information on all of the courses and pro playing tips. Keen golfers should also consider the option of accommodation at a 'Golf Hotel'. Typically these are establishments very close to the top golf courses that offer free (or heavily discounted) golf on courses that may otherwise be difficult to get a game on. They also arrange golf tournaments among their guests.

Horseback Riding. Whether you're looking for pony rides for children, treks for the competent or hacks for the inexperienced, the mixed terrain of beaches, rolling hills and woods makes riding in the Algarve a delight. Most of the horses you'll encounter are at least part Lusitano, a famous and sure-footed Portuguese breed. **Paraíso dos Cavalos** (Estrada de Almancil/Quinta do Lago; Tel.

Golf Deals

Algarve Golf can arrange discount rates and various packages and will provide vouchers to be collected at Faro airport. There are also packages for playing all the courses at Vilamoura – 5 rounds in 7 days, €325; 7 rounds in 10 days, €419. <www.algarvegolf.net>

289/394 189) is highly regarded and offers a friendly and professional service. The **Quinta do Lago Riding Centre**, at Quinta do Lago near the Ria Formosa Nature Preserve, (Tel. 289/396 099) is also recommended, as are the schools at **Quinta Penedo** (in Vale Fuzeiros, near Albufeira; Tel. 282/332 466),); **Vale de Ferro** (Mexilhoeira Grande between Lagos and Praia da Rocha); and at **Vale Navio** (Albufeira). Also consider **Centro Hípico Coca Maravilhas** (Tel. 282/491 840), north of Portimão and **Tiffany's Riding Centre,** Vale Grifo, Almadena (between Sagres and Lagos); Tel. 282/697 395).

Tennis. The most prestigious complex on the Algarve is the centre at **Vale do Lobo** (Tel. 289/357 850), which has 14 all-weather courts, including six that are floodlit. Close by is the well-equipped **Vilamoura Tennis Centre** (Tel. 289/302 369), which has 12 courts. The **Jim Stewart Tennis Academy** at Quinta do Lago (Tel. 289/398 848) has weekly coaching programmes on 5 hard and 2 synthetic grass courts. Others include the **Clube de Ténis Rocha Brava** at Praia do Carvoeiro (Tel. 282/358 856) with four courts and offering tuition and hire of equipment. The neighbouring **Carvoeiro Clube de Ténis** (Tel. 282/357 847) has 12 courts.

Hotels with a good number of courts include the Alfa Mar, Praia da Falésia, near Olhos de Agua (18 courts); Hotel Alvor Praia (7 courts); and Hotel Montechoro, near Albufeira (8 courts). Instruction in the pleasant surroundings of the Ocean Club at Luz (3 courts) is demanding but rewarding. Portimão has 7 municipal hard courts available to guests (Tel. 282/418 780 for booking).

Walking. The beaches and cliffs along the coast are excellent for walking, as are the mountains of the Serra do Monchique. A particularly good area for energetic walkers is near Praia da Luz, where you can climb 109 m (358 ft) from the beach or walk 3km (2 miles) to Porto de Mós or another 5 km (3 miles) to Ponta da Piedade, near Lagos. A new long-distance footpath, the Via Algarviana, is being developed and will eventually link Cabo S. Vicente with the Spanish border.

Spectator sports

Bullfights. The term 'bullfight' is rather inaccurate, for this is much less an actual duel between man and beast than a brutal ritual, the outcome of which never differs. The main difference between the Portuguese and Spanish *corrida*, however, is that in Portugal the bull leaves the ring bloodied but alive. Death does not come in the afternoon, but the following morning in the slaughterhouse. The Portuguese version is further sanitized in that the bull's horns are blunted in order to reduce the risk of injury (to men and horses) by goring.

If you want the colour, spectacle and strategy of the bullfight but would prefer not to see the *coup de grâce*, then the Portuguese version may suit you. Be aware, though, that there is still a lot of blood, and the whole episode may well prove extremely distasteful. Like the Spanish version, the bull is used as a pincushion for long darts, then taunted and run to the ground. Bullfights are held most Saturdays, almost entirely for the benefit of curious tourists, at Lagos, Quarteira, and Vila Real de Santo António, and Albufeira. Look for notices advertising 'Praça de Touros'. The one in Albufeira, one of the best attended, is called **Areias de São João** (Tel. 289/510 280).

Soccer (football). The Portuguese are wild about *futebol*, as they call it. The biggest clubs are from the two major cities, Lisbon and Oporto, but the Algarve has a team in Farense, from the regional capital. Check with the tourism office there for a schedule of matches.

CHILDREN'S ALGARVE

The beaches of the Algarve, with long, sandy, gently shelving beaches for small children, and small rocky coves ideal for older children to explore, are perfect for family holidays. Pay attention to the beach warning flags, however. Green means the sea is calm and a lifeguard is on duty; green plus a checkered flag means that the life-guard is not on duty; yellow urges caution; red means danger and warns bathers to stay ashore.

Waterparks are the most popular choice for children off the beach. There are several scattered across the Algarve; the best are reputed to be **Slide & Splash** (EN-125 Vale de Deus, near Lagoa; Tel. 282/341 685) and **The Big One** (En-125, near Alcantarilha; Tel. 282/322 827). Both of these offer bus service all day from many points along the Algarve. **Atlantic Park** (Quatro Estradas, near Quarteira) has an attractive mountain backdrop and features a daily high-diving show. Its neighbour, **Aquashow**, has fewer aqua thrills, but both children and adults get the chance to drive scaled-down Formula 1 cars on a mini racing circuit (adults need driving licences).

Krazy World (along the Algoz-Messines road, north of Albufeira; Tel. 282/574 134) has a miniature golf course, pet farm and pools. One of the newest family venues is **Montechoro Park**, which has an 18-hole mini-golf course, an Olympic-size swimming pool and many other facilities. Another attraction is **Zoomarine** (EN-125, km 65; Tel. 289/560 301), a small amusement park with performing dolphins and sea lions, a parrot show, a mini-zoo, a cinema, various children's fairground rides and swimming pools.

For older children, sports such as tennis, horseback riding, windsurfing and even golf may prove to be excellent diversions.

Several hotels in the Algarve are popular with families and well equipped for entertaining children. Most hotels in the Pestana chain, for example, have full 'Kids Club' programmes (with reading, treasure hunts, outdoor games etc). Perhaps the best setup of all is the huge playground and day school at the upscale **Sheraton Algarve** on Praia da Falésia. The hotel is one of the region's most luxurious, but in this case the children get as much out of it as the parents.

Calendar of events

Feb–March	Carnival (parades and processions), Loulé
February	Portugal Open (golf), Penina Golf
April	Mãe Soberana, Loulé (Pilgrimage to Nossa Senhora da Piedade)
May–June	International Music Festival of the Algarve
July	International Beer Festival (Silves Castle)
	International Jazz Festival (Loulé)
	Senhora do Carmo Festivities and Fair, Faro
August	Shellfish Festival (Olhão)
	Sardine Festival (Pinhal do Forte Novo, Quarteira
	Senhora dos Mártires Festivities and Fair, Castro Marim
September	Handcrafts Fair (Silves)
	Fishermen's Festivals (Albufeira)
	National Folklore Festival (folk music and dance), throughout Algarve
October	Religious and Trade Fairs (feiras) throughout Algarve
November	TAP Air Portugal Open Golf Championships
December	Christmas choral concert (Igreja do Carmo, Tavira)

EATING OUT

Most Algarve cooking is as unaffected as a fisherman's barbecue: grilled or fried fish, chicken and steaks. Which is not to say the Portuguese are not inventive; you'll sample combinations such as clams and pork, sole and bananas, or pork and figs.

You'll also find the spicy taste of Portugal's former colonies has crept into the national cuisine. Chicken *piri-piri* (made from Angolan peppers) is a hot and very popular dish in the Algarve. Curries occasionally appear on the menu, originating from the former colony of Goa (in Southern India) or Africa.

But mostly, along the 160-km (100-mile) coast, you'll enjoy an excellent range of fresh fish and seafood. These items are no longer cheap, as much of it is now being brought in from distant waters. The humble but noble Portuguese sardine is an exception, and with a hunk of local rustic bread and a bottle of house wine, you can still feast well on a small budget.

Meal Times

Breakfast *(pequeno almoço)* is usually eaten any time up until about 10am. **Lunch** *(almoço)* is served from shortly after noon until 2.30pm, and **dinner** *(jantar)* runs from 7:30 to 10:00pm (or later in a *casa de fado*). Snacks between meals are usually taken at a *pastelaria* (pastry and cake shop), *salão de chá* (tea shop), or what the Portuguese call, in English, a *snack bar* – a stand-up counter selling sandwiches, savoury pastries and sweets.

Because lunch and dinner tend to be major events, you may prefer the kind of light breakfast the Portuguese eat: coffee, toast or rolls, butter and jam. Hotels usually provide large American-style buffets.

The grilled fresh sardines served at local restaurants are an especially tasty treat.

Starters

As soon as you sit down you will be served a pre-starter snack that may consist of bread, butter and a combination of olives, sardine paste and cream cheese (this isn't complimentary and will be on your bill as a cover charge).

Hearty starters always include a choice of soups – some vegetable soups, thickened with potatoes, can be almost a meal in themselves. Fish soup is variable but *gaspacho*, the Portuguese version of the cold Andalusian tomato-based soup, is usually good.

Fans of smoked food have two treats to look out for. The first is smoked ham *(presunto fumado)* – the best coming from Chaves, the northernmost province of Portugal (although Monchique ham is also highly regarded). The second is smoked swordfish *(espadarte fumado)*, which is a quite similar to smoked salmon but has a grainier texture and is less sweet. Most restaurants also have a range of international starters.

Fish and Seafood

Besides sardines, tuna is the top fish along the Algarve. It is usually served as a steak, with almonds, or in a thick stew *(estufado)*. Prawns, crabs, lobsters and fresh fish are always their own best advertisement, and you will see them all over the Algarve either refrigerated in a window display or, in the case of large shellfish, counting their days in an aquarium waiting for your selection. Most shellfish and some fish are sold on a price per kilogram basis.

Beware that if you choose lobster, it may be brought to your table alive and very much kicking, for your seal of approval. Fish priced on a weight basis are also often brought to the table for a preview (though not alive). Unless you happen to be on expense account, this is the moment to ask the exact cost. Large shellfish can be very expensive, so make sure you get a proper answer to avoid problems when the bill arrives. There are two kinds of lobster: a *lavagante* (with large front claws) and the *lagostim* or *lagosta* (the spiny lobster or crayfish, without claws). Similarly, there are two kinds of crab; the *sapateira* is a big Atlantic type, the *santola* is a spider crab.

Look out for the following regional seafood dishes:

Açorda de marisco. A spicy, garlic-flavoured bread and seafood soup baked in a casserole, with raw eggs folded into the mixture at the table (also served as a starter).

Amêijoas à bulhão pato. Clams, fried or steamed with garlic and coriander.

Arroz de marisco. Seafood risotto.

Nearly every restaurant in Portugal serves a *couvert* (literally, cover) – an assortment of appetizers, including bread and butter, that appear to be free but are usually not. Your bill will include a charge of anywhere from €2 to €5 for the items. Theoretically, if you don't touch them, you shouldn't be charged for them – though you will probably have to point this out, since nearly everyone automatically eats them.

Bacalhau. Cod; pretty much the national dish of Portugal. The Portuguese have been drying and salting cod since their first sea voyages to Newfoundland in 1501. Strangely, even

> A menu that quotes a price as preço V. means variable, or market price. Clarify the day's market price before ordering.

though fresh fish is available on their own doorstep, they still prefer to ship in this relatively expensive, preserved fish. Preserving gives it a fuller flavour (though this is not always apparent when it is casseroled with many other ingredients). There are dozens of recipes for *bacalhau,* the most common on the Algarve being *à brás* – fried with onions and potatoes, then baked with a topping of beaten eggs.

Bife de Atum. A beefy fillet of tuna steak, marinated in wine or vinegar, salt, garlic and bay leaves, then cooked with onion and perhaps bacon.

Caldeirada de peixe. The Algarve version of the French bouillabaisse, a rich, filling mixed fish stew including potatoes, onions, tomatoes, peppers, wine and spices.

Cataplana. The region's most individual dish, named after the wok-like, copper pressure-cooker in which it is prepared. You may encounter several versions of the dish, but it is basically a combination of seafood, which always includes clams (*amêijoas*), plus salami-style sausage, ham, onion, garlic, paprika, a little chilli, parsley and white wine.

Choquinhos con tinta. Cuttlefish served in their own ink.

Espadarte. Swordfish, often grilled in a steak. On some menus it's listed as *peixe agulha*. Don't confuse it with *peixe espada*, a long thin fish, usually translated as 'scabbard fish'.

Salada de polvo. Octopus salad.

Sardinhas. The best-value fish dish you'll enjoy on the Algarve; plump, juicy, crisply grilled and served with boiled

A dockside restaurant in Portimão, advertising grilled sardines, is a natural choice for all types of seafood lovers.

potatoes. Note that fresh sardines are only available from June to October, though at Portimão you will get them year-round.

Meat and Poultry

Cabrito assado (no forno). Baked kid; not a common dish, but worth seeking out. *Cabrito estufado* is kid stewed with tomatoes and vegetables.

Carne de porco com amêijoas. An improbable but excellent combination of clams and roast pork, probably invented in the Alentejo, but adopted by the Algarve.

Favas à Algarvia. Pork and broad bean stew.

Feijoada. A hearty Brazilian dish consisting of dried beans and cabbage stewed with pork, sausage, bacon and whatever else of the pig is at hand (often the feet).

Frango piri-piri. What you most need to know about a *piri-piri* preparation is that it's hot. Chicken, usually, is cooked or basted with tiny red chilli peppers from Angola (you'll see them strung as necklaces in the market).

Galinha cerejada. Roast chicken served with smoked meats and rice.

Leitão. Roast suckling pig, served hot or cold.

Bife/Steak à Portuguêsa. Steak fried with garlic, topped with ham and a fried egg, and served in a casserole dish surrounded by sautéed potatoes.

Dessert

The Algarve, with a ready supply of almonds and figs, excels at sweet desserts. Both are employed in a variety of cakes

Produce markets will always have the freshest vegetables on hand, providing a taste of the Mediterranean climate.

and tarts, including *tarte de amêndoa,* almond tart. Other sweets worth trying are *arroz doce,* rice pudding topped with cinnamon; and *pudim flan,* crème caramel.

Portuguese cheese *(queijo)* is also an excellent dessert. The richest is *serra da estrela,* cured ewe's milk cheese from the country's highest mountain range. It takes some three hours to make each small cheese by hand and it is only available from December to April. Outside of this you'll have to make do with *tipo serra*, a harder, factory-made cheese. Other cheeses include *flamengo* (similar to Edam) and *saloio*, a creamy type of cottage cheese.

> Salt and pepper are seldom placed on the table. You will be given them if you ask, though: *sal e pimenta, faz favor*.

Table Wines

Portuguese wines, while not as well known as those from Spain and France, are uniformly good, and several regions produce truly excellent wines. You need only tell the waiter *tinto* (red) or *branco* (white) and you can't go wrong.

Vinho verde (green wine), produced in northwest Portugal, is a young white wine, slightly fizzy, light and delightful. A lesser known type is red wine from the same region, bearing the seemingly oxymoronic name *vinho verde tinto* (red green wine). Both of these wines should be served chilled, as should Portuguese rosé, which is also slightly bubbly and may be either sweet or very dry. *Vinhos maduros* are mature, or aged, wines.

Vinho espumante is Portuguese sparkling wine, packaged in a Champagne-shaped bottle. Most are sweet but you can also find some quite dry versions.

Several of the best wine-producing regions have names whose use is controlled by law *(região demarcada)*. The Dão and Douro in the north of Portugal produce vigorous reds and

There is no shortage of seafood restaurants by the docks of Portimão; they are a natural part of the landscape.

flavoursome whites. Wines from the Alentejo are also highly regarded. Of the local wines, you are most likely to see the Lagoa label, packing more of a punch than average wine.

Other Alcoholic Drinks

The two most celebrated Portuguese wines, port and Madeira, are mostly known as dessert wines, but they may also be sipped as aperitifs. The before-dinner varieties are dry or extra dry white port, and the dry Madeiras, *Sercial* and *Verdelho*. These should be served slightly chilled. After dinner, sip one of the famous ruby or tawny ports (aged tawnys are especially good) or a Madeira dessert wine, *Boal* or *Malvasia* (Malmsey). Two local wines that make excellent aperitifs are *Algar Seco* and *Afonso III*. Reminiscent of sherry, both come from Lagoa and are served chilled.

Local after-dinner specialties include *aguardente de medronho,* a brandy distilled from the fruit of the arbutus

tree. Blended with honey, it's called *medronheira de mel.*
Equally powerful is *bagaço,* or *bagaceira,* a firewater made
from grape residue in the same way as the French make *marc*
and the Italians *grappa.*

Portuguese beers are good and refreshing. Light or dark,
they are served chilled, bottled or from the tap. One of the
best and most common is Sagres.

Coffee and Tea

Most Portuguese order a *bica* when they want a coffee, which
is a small espresso. If that's too small
for you, order a *duplo,* a double.
Take one *bica,* add water, and you
have a *carioca*; a few drops of milk transforms it into a *garoto.*

> **May I have the bill?**
> *A conta, se faz favor?*

A white coffee in a café is a *galão,* served in a tall glass. In
a restaurant you would order a *café com leite.* Tea (*chá*) has
been drunk in Portugal as long as it has been known to the
western world.

To Help You Order…

We'd like a table?	**Queríamos uma mesa.**		
I'd like a/an/some …	**Queria …**		
beer	**cerveja**	fish	**peixe**
mineral water	**água mineral**	rice	**arroz**
(sparkling)	**com gás**	fruit	**fruta**
(still)	**sem gás**	salad	**salada**
bill	**a conta**	ice cream	**gelado**
bread	**pão**	salt	**sal**
butter	**manteiga**	meat	**carne**
napkin	**guardanapo**	sandwich	**sanduíche**
menu	**ementa**	coffee	**um café**
soup	**sopa**	pepper	**pimenta**
milk	**leite**	dessert	**sobre mesa**

sugar	**açúcar**	tea	**chá**
potatoes	**batatas**	wine	**vinho**

...and Read the Menu

alho	garlic	**frito**	fried
amêijoas	baby clams	**guisado**	stew
assado	roast	**laranja**	orange
atun	tuna	**legumes**	vegetables
azeitonas	olives	**leitão**	suckling pig
bacalhau	cod (salted)	**linguado**	sole
besugo	sea-bream	**lombo**	fillet
bife (vaca)	steak (beef)	**lulas**	squid
bolo	cake	**maçã**	apple
borrego	lamb	**mariscos**	shellfish
cabrito	kid	**melancia**	watermelon
camarões	shrimp	**mexilhões**	mussels
caranguejo	crab	**molho**	sauce
cavala	mackerel	**morangos**	strawberries
cebola	onion	**ostras**	oysters
chouriço	spicy sausage	**ovo**	egg
churrasco	grilled meat	**pargo**	bream
coelho	rabbit	**pescada**	hake
cogumelos	mushrooms	**pescadinha**	whiting
costeletas	chops	**pêssego**	peach
couve	cabbage	**porco**	pork
cozido	boiled	**presunto**	smoked ham
dobrada	tripe	**queijo**	cheese
enguias, eiros	eels	**robalo**	bass
estufado	stewed/braised	**salsichão**	large sausage
feijões	beans	**sardinhas**	sardines
figos	figs	**torrada**	toast
framboesas	raspberries	**uvas**	grapes
frango	chicken	**vitela**	veal

HANDY TRAVEL TIPS

An A–Z Summary of Practical Information

Algarve

A

ACCOMMODATION (See also CAMPING on page 103, YOUTH HOSTELS on page 126 and the list of hotels on pages 127–135)

Besides hotels, which range in an official category from 1 to 5 stars (not directly related to price), you'll find *aparthotels* (1- or 2-bedroom with kitchenette, occasionally called *aldeamentos*) as well as a selection of inns variously categorized by overlapping and confusing, names. A small, basic inn is labelled a *pensao* or *residencial* (pension); *quinta* and *estalagem* refer to an inn or rural estate, and *albergaria* is generally a 4–5 star inn. A *pousada* is a government-owned and -operated inn, often but not always in an historic building. There are just two in the Algarve, in Sagres and Sao Brás de Alportel, but look for a couple more to be opened – in the Palace of Estói and a former convent near the castle in Tavira – in near future.

Many tour operators book blocks at large, modern (and often undistinguished) hotels on or near beaches. If you wish to be on the beach, make sure that what is described as a 'sea view' is not one that requires binoculars to see the distant ocean.

I'd like a single/double room.	**Queria um quarto simples/duplo.**
with bath/shower	**com banho/chuveiro**
What's the rate per night?	**Qual é o preço por noite?**

AIRPORT (*aeroporto*)

Faro International Airport, serving the Algarve, is 7 km (4 miles) from Faro, the regional capital. It's just a 10-minute taxi ride to Faro, and about half an hour by car to Albufeira. There's also a bus service to Faro. Several international and local car rental agencies have service desks at the airport. Helpful staff at the airport tourist information office will assist you with finding accommodation and any other queries you may have. Elsewhere in the terminal are a post office, bank, ATM machine, restaurant and bar, newsstand, souvenir shop and duty-free shop.

Airport Information: Tel. 289/800 800 (arrival and departure times, Tel. 289/800 801).

TAP Air Portugal reservations: Tel. 289/800 731

PGA Portugalia reservations: Tel. 289/800 851

Where can I get a taxi?	**Onde posso encontrar um taxi?**
Please take these bags.	**Leve-me a baggagem, por favor.**

B

BICYCLE RENTAL (aluguer de bicicleta)

Virtually every resort hotel of size will have bicycles available for rent. If yours does not, the major resorts all have scooter and bike rental shops. Among those are Quiosqe Navegador, in Sagres (Rua Comandante Matoso; Tel. 282/624 751), Mourabike in Vilamoura (Tel. 91/727 0801) and Motoride in Lagos (Rua José Afonso, 23; Tel. 282/761 720). Expect to pay about €8.50–€10 per day.

BUDGETING FOR YOUR TRIP

With a favourable exchange rate, the Algarve may well be cheaper than many other European beach destinations. However, the season when you go will have much to do with the cost of your trip. Hotel rates rise astonishingly during the summer months.

Getting to the Algarve. Many Europeans fly direct to Faro aboard regularly scheduled and charter flights. Scheduled flights from England and continental Europe may cost anywhere from €300–€600 roundtrip. For those travelling from beyond Europe, the flight will be a higher proportion of your overall budget – though scheduled flights from North America can often be had for €500–€600 roundtrip, outside the high season. Economical package deals – airline and hotel – are usually available. For low cost fares try easyJet and Virgin Express.

Algarve

Accommodation. Hotels at the top levels are comparable to large European cities. There is a huge difference in full rates according to season. In high summer season (July–August especially), hotel prices are exorbitant – often double what they cost in off-season. Outside high season, many hotels at the two-, three- and four-star ratings are excellent value. In high season, a double room with bath per night in a 3-star hotel averages €55–80; 4-star hotel, €90–130; 5-star hotel, €180–400. *Pousadas* generally range from €130–160 for a double room.

Meals. Even top-rated restaurants may be surprisingly affordable compared to most European cities. Portuguese wines are quite good and very attractively priced, even in fine restaurants. A 3-course meal with wine in a reasonable establishment averages about €15–30 per person. Most hotels offer half- and full-board plans. Continental or full buffet breakfast is nearly always included in the price of hotels.

Local transport. Buses and taxis are reasonably priced. Local buses are less than €2; a taxi costs between €3–10 for most fares within a resort or town (a supplement of 20% is levied on weekends, public holidays and between 10pm and 6am). Taxis can be hired for day trips for set fees; check with the local tourist office for a list of trips.

Incidentals. Your major expenses will probably be excursions, sporting activities and entertainment, unless these are included in the hotel or package deal.

Renting a car to get around is a good idea to allow maximum flexibility, but be sure to budget for the cost of fuel, which is costly, as in most of Europe. Economy car rental is cheaper than in most parts of Europe; expect it to run between €30–50 per day (including collision insurance and taxes). You may find even better bargains at local firms. Fuel per litre costs €1.10 for unleaded, €0.90 for diesel.

Organized excursions (day trips including lunch) costs average: Monchique/Silves €35, Loulé/Alte (half day) €20; jeep safari, €40.

Expect to pay about €50–100 for *golf* for an 18-hole championship course (or €40 for 9 holes); €65–80 per day for *big-game fishing* (spectators €50); *horseback riding,* €15–25 per hour; and *tennis* €6 per hour; Instruction for most sports ranges from €25–30 per hour.

Nightlife and entertainment costs vary widely. Expect cover fees at discos to range from €7.50–15 escudos (usually includes first drink); casino entrance, €15. Entrance to waterparks generally cost around €13 for adults and €8 for children.

C

CAMPING *(campismo)*

Many of the Algarve's two dozen camping sites are within easy reach of a beach. They range from very cheap, basic grounds to vast recreational centres with restaurants, pools and sports facilities. Sites belonging to clubs or the Portuguese Camping Federation are open to holders of a Camping Carnet. There are also a number of private sites that may only be used by members of the respective owners' associations.

Camping on beaches, or indeed anywhere outside recognized sites, is illegal. Details on all Algarve campsites are available from tourist information offices or the Federação Portuguesa de Campismo (Av. Coronel Eduardo Galhardo, 24-D, Lisbon; Tel. 218/126 890, fax 218/126 918). Check the web site <www.portugal-insite.pt> for a detailed list of 20 campsites throughout the Algarve (click on the individual site for features).

Costs range from €5 per person with tent and €7 per caravan/trailer.

Is there a campsite near here?	**Há algum parque de campismo por aqui perto?**
May we camp here?	**Podemos acampar aqui?**
We have a caravan (trailer).	**Temos uma caravana.**

Algarve

CAR RENTAL/HIRE *(de aluguer)* (See also DRIVING on page 107)
Local car rental firms compete with the major international organizations at Faro Airport and all principal resorts. Prices are usually similar, but some small local agencies occasionally feature very inexpensive daily and weekly rates.

You must be at least 21 and have held a valid national (or international) driving licence for at least one year. Rental companies will accept your home country national driver's licence. Third-party insurance is included in the basic charge but a collision damage waiver (CDW) and personal accident policy may be added. You will need to present a recognized credit card or a significant cash deposit when booking.

A value-added tax (IVA) is added to the total charge, but will have been included if you have pre-paid the car hire before arrival (normally the way to obtain the lowest rates). Third-party insurance is required and included, but full collision coverage is advisable as well. Many credit cards automatically include this if you use the card to pay for the car, but be sure to verify this before departure. Renting at an airport may incur a surcharge.

Check that the agreement covers driving in Spain if you intend going there. A basic economy car is likely to average between €30–50 per day (including collision insurance and taxes).

I'd like to hire a car today/ tomorrow.	**Queria alugar um carro para hoje/amanhã.**
for one day/a week	**por um dia/uma semana**
Please include full insurance.	**Que inclua um seguro contra todos os riscos, por favor.**

CLIMATE

The Algarve's climate is generally warm all year round, with rare extremes. Winter evenings can occasionally be rather chilly, and hot periods in July and August may prove stifling to those who prefer milder weather. Spring and autumn are the best seasons to travel in the Algarve.

Air temperature

	J	F	M	A	M	J	J	A	S	O	N	D
°C	12	12	14	15	18	21	23	24	22	18	15	13
°F	54	54	57	59	64	69	73	75	72	64	59	55

Sea temperature

°C	15	16	17	18	19	21	21	20	19	18	16	14
°F	59	61	62	64	66	69	69	67	66	64	61	57

CLOTHING (*roupa*)

As a resort area extremely popular with beach and sports enthusiasts, dress is casual in almost all parts of the Algarve. The exceptions are certain luxury hotels and restaurants, as well as casinos, where smart (though never formal) attire is appreciated.

Pack a sweater or jacket, even in summer, as evenings can turn quite cool. Winters are mild with the occasional shower, so a light rainproof jacket may come in handy. It's cooler in the mountains and also in Lisbon and its environs, so dress warmer if you plan on including these.

Will I need a tie?	**É preciso gravata?**
Is it all right if I wear this?	**Vou bem assim?**

CRIME AND SAFETY (*segurança*) (See also Emergencies and Police on pages 111 and 119)

As a major tourist area, the Algarve experiences more petty crime than other parts of Portugal, though crimes involving violence against tourists are very rare. Theft from rental cars is the most common crime targeting tourists. In rural areas the problem is far less acute, but in resorts and where cars are left unattended for a period of time (at beach parking lots, beauty spots, etc.) the risk is high.

Burglaries of holiday apartments, though less common than car theft, also occur, so be on your guard to the best extent possible.

As a general rule, never leave anything in your car, even if it is out of sight and locked in the boot. Keep valuables in the hotel safe and refrain from carrying large sums of money or expensive jewellery on the street. Do not leave bags and cameras unattended on the beach.

Report any theft to the hotel receptionist, the nearest police station, or the local tourist office. You must report any losses to the local police within 24 hours and obtain a copy of your statement for insurance purposes.

If you are going to Lisbon, beware that the city is infamous for its pickpockets, particularly on the metro, the buses and Rossio square. You are also advised not to walk in the Bairro Alto or Alfama areas at night unless in a group.

I want to report a theft.	**Quero participar um roubo.**

CUSTOMS AND ENTRY REQUIREMENTS *(alfândega)*

Americans, British, Canadians and many other nationalities need only a valid passport – no visa – to visit Portugal. EU nationals may enter with an identity card. The length of stay authorized for most tourists is 90 days (60 for US and Canadian citizens).

The Portuguese-Spanish border scarcely serves as frontier anymore and visitors can come and go easily, though you should carry identification.

Currency restrictions. Visitors from within the EU can bring in or exit with any amount of local or foreign currency into Portugal, but sums exceeding the equivalent of €5,000 in foreign currency from outside the EU should be declared on arrival.

Customs. Free exchange of non-duty-free goods for personal use is permitted between Portugal and other EU countries. However, duty-free items still are subject to restrictions: check before you go.

I've nothing to declare.	**Não tenho nada a declarar.**
It's for my personal use.	**É para uso pessoal.**

D

DRIVING (See also Car Rental on page 104 and Emergencies on page 111)

Driving can be the best way to see the Algarve, but, especially in high season, traffic can test one's patience. It can also be costly, as petrol and rental charges are likely to outpace the cost of public transport.

Road conditions. The southern Algarve coastline is served by the Estrada Nacional 125 (abbreviated to the 'EN 125'). Parallel to this road is a new motorway (the Via do Infante), which runs from Spain as far west as Lagos. This road links in with the A2 motorway going north to Lisbon. The Via do Infante has helped divert traffic from the EN 125, which in summer can become a bumper-to-bumper nightmare. Exercise care at all times on this road; the accident rate is high.

In rural areas, beware of such rustic hazards as herds of sheep or goats around the next bend, unlit donkeys and carts at night, tractors, hay carts, etc. If driving to Lisbon, allow at least 3 hours. In high season the motorway can be quite congested, and once you reach the centre of Lisbon traffic slows to a crawl.

Rules and Regulations. The rules of the road are the same as in most western European countries. At roundabouts the vehicle on the roundabout has priority unless road markings or lights indicate otherwise. Local driving standards are improving but are still erratic. Speed limits are 120kph (75mph) on motorways, 90kph (56mph) on other roads and 50kph (37mph) in urban areas. Cars towing caravans (trailers) are restricted to 50kph (31mph) in towns and 70kph (45mph) on the open road and highways. Most highways have tolls *(portagems)*. The Portuguese routinely appear to disregard speed limits, but that doesn't mean you should.

Seat belts are mandatory, and children under 12 cannot sit in the front seat unless strapped into a special child restraint. You can be fined on the spot for not carrying your licence, passport, or car-rental documents; for ignoring parking restrictions; and for drink-driving (limit 0.5mg/l).

If you take your own car, you need only your national driving licence, car registration papers and the Green Card extension to your insurance – third party is obligatory, and comprehensive coverage is highly recommended. A warning triangle is also compulsory.

Fuel Costs. Fuel by the litre is expensive in Portugal, as it is throughout Western Europe. At the time of going to press, fuel per litre costs €1.10 for unleaded, €0.90 for diesel. Prices, controlled by the government, should be the same – or very close to it – everywhere you go. Many petrol stations are 24-hour, and all accept credit cards.

Parking. Parking in most towns and resorts is manageable. Don't disregard no-parking signs: your car may be towed away. Certain areas are metred and others are 'Blue Zones' where you must buy a ticket from a machine. Car parks and garages are also available.

If You Need Help. There are SOS telephones stationed about every 3 km (2 miles) on main roads. If you belong to a motoring organisation affiliated with the Automóvel Clube de Portugal (in Lisbon, Rua Rosa Araújo 24; Tel. 213/180 100), you can make use of their services free of charge. The emergency number for police and ambulance is Tel. 112.

Road signs. Standard international pictograms are used in Portugal, but you might also encounter the following signs:

Alto/Stop	Halt
Cruzamento	Crossroads
Curva perigosa	Dangerous bend
Descida ingreme	Steep hill
Desvio	Diversion
Encruzilhada	Crossroads
Estacionamento permitido	Parking allowed

Estacionamento proíbido	No parking
Guiar com cuidado	Drive with care
Obras/Fim de obras	Road works (men working)/ end of road works
Paragem de autocarro	Bus stop
Pare	Stop
Passagem proíbida	No entry
Pedestres/peões	Pedestrians
Perigo	Danger
Posto de socorros	First-aid post
Proibida a entrada	No entry
Saída de camiões	Lorry (truck) exit
Seguir pela direita/esquerda	Keep right/left
Sem saída	No through road
Sentido proíbido	No entry
Sentido único	One-way street
Silêncio	Silence zone
Stop	Stop
Trabalhos	Road works (men working)
Trânsito proíbido	No through traffic
Veículos pesados	Heavy vehicles
Velocidade máxima	Maximum speed

Are we on the right road for …?	**É esta a estrada para …?**
Fill the tank, please, super.	**Encha o depósito de super, por favor.**
Check the oil/tyres/ battery, please.	**Verifique o óleo/os pneus/ a bateria, se faz favor.**
I've broken down.	**O meu carro está avariado.**
There's been an accident.	**Houve um acidente.**

E

ELECTRICITY *(electricidade, luz)*

Standard throughout Portugal is 220-volt, 50-cycle AC. For US appliances, 220v transformers and plug adaptors are needed.

| I need an adaptor/ a battery, please. | **Preciso de um adaptador/ uma pilha, por favor.** |

EMBASSIES/CONSULATES/HIGH COMMISSIONS
(embaixada; consulado)

A number of European countries have consuls or honorary consuls in the Algarve.

British consulate (Consulado da Grã Bretanha, which handles Commonwealth nationals): Largo Francisco A Maurício, 7-1; Portimão; Tel. 282/417 800.

Canadian consulate (Consulado de Canadá): Rua Aboim Ascensão, 87; Faro; Tel. 289/803 757).

Embassies in Lisbon:

Australia: Av. da Liberdade 200; Tel. 213/101 500.

Canada (Embassy/Consulate): Av. da Liberdade 144, 3°; Tel. 213/164 600.

Republic of Ireland (Embassy/Consulate): Rua da Imprensa à Estrela 1; Tel. 213/929 440.

South Africa (Embassy): Avenida Luís Bivar 10/10 A; Tel. 213/192 200.

United Kingdom (Embassy): Rua de São Bernardo 33; Tel. 213/ 924 000.

USA (Embassy/Consulate): Avenida das Forças Armadas 16; Tel. 217/273 300.

Most embassies and consulates are open Mon–Fri from 9 or 10am until 5pm, with a break in the middle of the day of 1–2 ½ hours.

EMERGENCIES *(urgência)*

Dial 112 for medical, police and general emergencies in all Portugal.

The hospitals at Faro and Portimão have *bancos de urgência* (emergency wards). Some hospitals can also handle dental emergencies. For trouble on the road such as a breakdown, see DRIVING on page 107.

G

GAY & LESBIAN TRAVELLERS

In a country heavily influenced by the Catholic Church, attitudes towards gays are not as tolerant as elsewhere in Europe, though in tourist-dominated enclaves of the Algarve, such as 'the Strip' in Albufeira, gay travellers will find accommodating bars and restaurants. A web site, <www.portugalgay.pt>, contains a travel guide with information in English and other languages. It has some specific information relating to the Algarve and a message board.

GETTING TO THE ALGARVE (See also AIRPORT on page 100)

Air Travel. There are regular scheduled, cheap charter flights to Faro (mostly in summer) from the UK, Ireland and most major cities in Western Europe. Scheduled flights by TAP Air Portugal and British Airways are more expensive, though they usually offer special deals outside high season.

TAP/Air Portugal (Tel. 707/205 700 anywhere in Portugal; Lisbon, 21/841 69 90; New York, 212/969-5775; London, 0845/601 0932) is the national Portuguese airline. From the US to Lisbon, it flies direct daily from New York and Newark, and once a week from Boston. Continental flies direct to Lisbon from Newark and TWA flies from New York's JFK airport. These and many other airlines make connections in Lisbon and travel on to Faro. Travellers originating their journeys in Canada, Australia, New Zealand or South

Algarve

Africa will connect to Lisbon or Faro in London or another major European city.

Faro International Airport is 7 km (4 miles) from Faro, the regional capital. Airport information is: Tel. 289/800 800

By Car. Many travellers each year, arriving for long stays in Portugal, take their cars from other points in Europe by major highways through Spain and Portugal. British travellers can take their car across the Channel to France or Belgium and make the drive from there, although the trip is likely to last 3 or 4 days. See the information below on ferries, under 'By Sea'.

The main access road to Lisbon and the Algarve from France, through Spain, is at the western end of the Pyrenees. A motorway runs from Biarritz (France) to Burgos. From there, take the N1 to Madrid and continue on the E4 via Badajoz and Setúbal, or the E4 to Mérida and then go via the E102 through Seville. As the distance from Calais to the Algarve is over 2,000 km (1,300 miles), you might like to consider the long-distance car ferry service from Plymouth to Santander in northern Spain (a 24-hour trip). From Santander follow the N611 and then the E3 via Valladolid and Coimbra.

By Rail. Portugal is linked to the European railway network; connections to Lisbon are possible from points throughout Spain, France and the rest of continental Europe. Travel to Portugal is included on any InterRail or EurailPass; the Eurodomino pass is available for travel within Portugal only for a 3-, 5- or 10-day period, but may not be as good a deal as it is on more expensive rail networks in northern Europe.

The Portuguese national railway network is called **Caminhos de Ferro Portugueses** (Tel. 808/208 208; <www.cp.pt>). The Santa Apolónia station in Lisbon (Avenida Dom Henrique) serves all international trains. Daily international trains run between Paris and Lisbon (Sud Express), crossing the frontier at Vilar Formoso; between Lisbon and Madrid, crossing the frontier at Marvão; and between Oporto and Vigo, crossing the frontier at Valença. Connecting trains to the Algarve depart from Lisbon's Terreiro do Paço via Barreiro, going to Lagos, Albufeira, Faro, Tavira and Vila Real, among others (though nothing west of Lagos); the trip to Faro, for example, takes between 4 and 6 hours, depending upon the type of train.

By Sea. Lisbon is a major port, and several cruise ships include a port-of-call in the capital, including Celebrity, Renaissance, Princess, Norwegian and Royal Caribbean. Ferries from Great Britain (Brittany Ferries) go to Santander, Spain from Plymouth and Portsmouth and to Bilbao, Spain from Portsmouth (P & O Ferries). Crossings range from 24 to 36 hours. The drive from northern Spain to the Algarve is then likely to take another 15 to 18 hours.

GUIDES AND TOURS *(guias; visitas guiadas)*

A number of guided day-trip itineraries are available through almost all hotels and a myriad of local travel agencies and tour operators. These include: Seville, Lisbon, the River Guadiana, Silves and Monchique, Sagres, Lagos and the west, Loulé market and Alte, and jeep safaris. If you would like a personal guide to a particular place, the nearest tourist office or travel agency should be able to direct you to qualified local guides. Day trips can be arranged with taxi drivers at set fees; again, see the local tourist information office for details.

Boat trips exploring the nooks and crannies of the famous Barlavento (west) coast are a popular choice; they depart from several points west of Vilamoura, most notably from Portimão.

Tourism offices in Albufeira, Tavira, Faro and São Brás de Alportel offer guided walks of the historical centres of towns.

Alternativ Tour (Tel. 96/500 4337) in Monchique offers ecological cycling and walking tours of the Serra de Monchique.

We'd like an English-speaking guide/an English interpreter.	**Queremos uma guia que fale inglês /um intérprete de inglês.**

H

HEALTH AND MEDICAL CARE (see also EMERGENCIES, page 111)
Standards of hygiene are generally very high; the most likely illness to
befall travellers will be due to an excess of sun or alcohol. The water
is safe to drink, but bottled water is always safest and is available everywhere. Even most local people drink bottled water, *água com gas* (car-
bonated) or *sem gas* (still). It is good, clean and inexpensive. Mosquitoes
are common in summer; an anti-mosquito device that plugs into your
wall and emits a vapour noxious to the insect, but not to you, is worth-
while and available at airport shops.

Farmácias (chemists) are open during normal business hours and are
recognizable by an illuminated green cross sign. At other times one shop
in each neighbourhood is on duty round the clock. Addresses are listed
in newspapers. To locate night pharmacies, call Tel. 118.

For more serious illness or injury, all principal Algarve towns and
resorts have hospitals, and many doctors are multilingual (most can
speak English remarkably well). There are also a number of expatriate
doctors at medical clinics and health centres throughout the region.
Tourist offices carry lists of English-speaking doctors. The Red Cross
(*Cruz Vermelha*) can be contacted in Faro (Tel. 289/899 900) and
Portimão (Tel. 282/485 640).

Medical insurance to cover illness or accident while abroad is a
good investment. EU nationals with the EU form E111 obtained well
before departure can receive free emergency treatment at Social
Security and Municipal hospitals in Portugal. Privately billed hospital
visits are expensive.

Where's the nearest (all night) pharmacy?	**Onde fica a farmácia (de serviço) mais próxima?**
I need a doctor/dentist.	**Preciso de um médico/uma dentista.**
I'm not feeling well.	**Não me sinto bem**

I've got a fever.	**Tenho febre.**
I have toothache.	**Tenho dor de dentes.**
an ambulance	**ambulância**
hospital	**hospital**
sunburn	**queimadura de sol**
sunstroke	**uma insolação**
a fever	**uma febre**
an upset stomach	**uma indigestão**
insect bite	**uma picadela de insecto**

HOLIDAYS *(feriado)*

National holidays:

1 January	*Ano Novo*	New Year's Day
25 April	*Dia da Liberdade*	Revolution Day
1 May	*Dia do Trabalho*	Labour Day
10 June	*Dia de Portugal*	National Day
15 August	*Assunção*	Assumption
5 October	*Heróis da República*	Republic Day
1 November	*Todos-os-Santos*	All Saints' Day
1 December	*Dia da Independência*	Independence Day
8 December	*Imaculada Conceição*	Immaculate Conception
25 December	*Natal*	Christmas Day

Movable dates:

Carnaval	Shrove Tuesday
Sexta-feira Santa	Good Friday
Corpo de Deus	Corpus Christi

In addition, every town closes down and takes to the streets at least once a year in honour of its own patron saint. See the Calendar of Events in 'What to Do' for other events.

Algarve

Are you open tomorrow?	**Estão abertos amanhã?**
When do you close?	**Quando fecha?**

L

LANGUAGE

Portuguese, a derivative of Latin, is spoken in such far-flung spots as Brazil, Angola, Mozambique and Macau – former colonies of Portugal. Your high-school Spanish may help with signs and menus, but will not unlock the mysteries of spoken Portuguese. The Portuguese in Portugal is much more closed and gutteral-sounding and is also spoken much faster than that in Brazil. A surprising number of people in the Algarve speak quite passable and even fluent English.

The *Berlitz Portuguese Phrasebook and Dictionary* covers most situations you're likely to encounter during a visit to Portugal.

M

MAPS

The Algarve is a relatively small region, linked east to west by the EN 125, so orientation is easy. The red-green-and-yellow 'Portugal Tourist Map', available at some tourist information offices, is a map of the entire country; you may need a magnifying glass for the smaller roads in the Algarve. Otherwise, to explore roads less travelled, the 'Turinta' map of the Algarve (1:128,000) is a good buy. All tourist information offices will supply you with a reasonable street plan of the local town.

a street map of...	**uma planta de...**
a road map of the Algarve	**um mapa das estradas do Algarve**

MEDIA *(jornal; revista)*

Europe's principal newspapers, including most British dailies, and the *International Herald Tribune*, are available on the day of publication at many newsagents and hotels. Popular foreign magazines are also sold at the same shops or stands. The most important Portuguese-language daily is *Diário de Notícias,* which contains full cultural listings. Popular foreign magazines and paperback books in English are also widely available.

English-language publications with useful information as to what's on (folklore, markets, music, cinema, sporting events, etc.) include: *The Algarve News*, a bi-weekly newspaper; the *Algarve Resident*, a weekly magazine; and *Welcome to the Algarve,* a monthly free newspaper/information sheet. *Algarve Tips,* a 150-page booklet distributed free of charge at many hotels, also has a wealth of useful listings.

There are two government-operated TV channels in Portugal. Most large hotels and some bars also have satellite TV showing feature films, football games and other big sporting events. Tune into Solar Radio (90.5 FM) for English news bulletins at 8:30am and also later in the day and KISS FM (101.2 FM) for hourly English news, a nightly 'English show' and rock and pop music from London.

Have you any English-language   **Tem jornais/revistas**
newspapers/magazines?   **em inglês?**

MONEY *(dinheiro)* (See also BUDGETING FOR YOUR TRIP on page 101)
Currency *(moeda).* The escudo was superceded by the euro in January 2002. The euro is divided into 100 cêntimos – the basic unit of currency. The smallest coin is the 1 cêntimo piece, and the largest is the 2 euro coin. Bank note denominations are: 5, 10, 20, 50 and 100 euros. The symbol for the euro is € and is written before the number of euros, eg €7.50 is 7 euros and 50 cêntimos.

Currency Exchange *(banco; câmbio).* Normal banking hours are Mon–Fri 8:30am–3pm. Some banks remain open later and at weekends to change money. There is also a 24-hour exchange office at the airport. Changing money can be quite expensive, and you are advised to check the rate of commission before any transaction. Banks levy a minimum charge of €2.50–5 for travellers cheques, so it is not a good idea to exchange small amounts with them. Automatic money-exchanging machines (ATMs) provide by far the best exchange rates.

At the time of going to press, US $1 = €1; £1 = €1.60.

Credit Cards *(cartão de crédito)*. Standard international credit cards are widely accepted. However, in some shops and restaurants, especially in small villages, you may not be able to use a credit card.

ATMs *(caixa automática)*. Automatic teller machines outside banks, identified by the MB (MultiBanco) sign, are widely available. You can get cash (maximum of €200 per day) with a Visa or Mastercard or other debit card on one of the international networks like Cirrus or Plus, provided you know the personal identification number (PIN). The PIN should be four digits.

Travellers Cheques. Less necessary now that ATMs have proliferated across the world, international travellers cheques (such as Thomas Cooke or American Express) can be cashed at any bank, though a high flat-rate fee is charged for changing them. Paying by cheque is invariably more expensive than by cash, due to the lower rate of exchange. You will need to show your passport.

Can I pay with this credit card? **Posso pagar com cartão de crédito?**

I want to change some pounds/dollars.	**Queria trocar libras/dólares.**
Can you cash a traveller's cheque?	**Pode pagar um cheque de viagem?**
Where's the nearest bank/ currency exchange office?	**Onde fica o banco mais próximo/a casa de câmbio mais próxima?**
How much is that?	**Quanto custa isto?**

O

OPENING HOURS *(horas de abertura)*
Most shops and offices open 9am–1pm and 3–7pm weekdays and
9am–1pm Saturday. Most museums are closed on Monday and
public holidays. On every other day (including Sunday) they are
open 10/11am–5pm, but most close noon–2pm or 1–2.30pm.

The Portuguese do not take a siesta, but most businesses close for
a 1–2 hour lunch break. **Banks** are open 8:30am to 3pm Monday–
Friday. In resorts many **bars** are open from noon (or earlier) until the
wee hours. Informal **restaurants** may open all day but more upscale
establishments may only open at lunch and in the evening, or for
dinner only. Some restaurants close one day a week, so it is a good
idea to check first with the establishment.

P

POLICE *(polícia)* (See also EMERGENCIES on page 111)
Police wearing armbands marked CD (it stands for Corpo Distrital,
meaning local corps) are assigned to assist tourists and normally
speak at least a smidgen of a foreign language. On highways, traffic
is controlled by the Guarda Nacional Republicana (GNR) in white
cars or on motorcycles. For a general emergency, dial Tel. 112.

Where's the nearest police station?	**Onde fica o posto de policia mais próximo?**
Police officer	**Senhor Guarda**

POST OFFICES *(correios)*
Post offices are indicated by the letters CTT (*Correios, Telegrafos e
Telefones*). The mail service is generally good, though it can get
bogged down during the height of the season. You can buy stamps
from most shops as well – they usually display a sign that says
Correios. Most mailboxes follow the British pillar-box design and are
painted bright red.

Algarve

Main offices are open 8.30am to 6.30 or 7pm Monday–Friday; local branches are open 9am to 12:30pm and 2 to 6pm Monday–Friday. The main post offices in Portimão and Faro open on Saturday mornings as well.

Sending a postcard or letter under 20 g anywhere within the EU costs €0.55; sending the same to the rest of the world costs €0.70. Mail from Portugal may take up to a week to reach a European destination. There is also a following-day 'Azul' (express) service.

Where's the nearest post office?	**Onde fica a estação de correios mais próxima?**
A stamp for this letter/postcard, please.	**Um selo para esta carta/este postal, por favor.**
express (special delivery)	**expresso**
airmail	**via aérea**
registered	**registado**

PUBLIC TRANSPORT

Buses (*autocarro*). EVA Transportes (<www.eva-transportes.pt>) operates most buses in the Algarve. A baffling variety of local and regional timetables may be consulted at any bus station or tourist information office. Most buses run on time. Buy your ticket on board the bus for all services except for the Algarve Express, where tickets must be purchased in advance at the station. Bus stops are denoted by the sign 'Paragem'.

Trains (*comboio*). An Algarve railway line runs from Lagos in the west to the eastern frontier at Vila Real de Santo António, with 50 stations in between. Stations are in or near Faro, Portimão and Lagos, but in other spots are far enough away to require a bus or taxi ride. The most notable example is the station of Albufeira, which is actually near Ferreiras and a good 15-minute bus ride from the resort. There is not a great deal of difference in time or price between long-distance buses and trains, but the latter offer superior scenery.

A railway line links the Algarve with Lisbon, terminating in the south side of the river Tagus (connecting ferry included in the fare). The fastest trains take just three hours to cover the distance between the Algarve junction Tunes and Barreiro, across the River Tagus from Lisbon.

Train schedules are posted at all railway stations; request a *guía de horarios* for a full listing of timetables. Consult the web site of Caminhos de Ferro Portugueses, the national railway network, for timetables and information on international and domestic trains: <www.cp.pt>.

Taxis *(táxi)*. Portuguese taxis are black with green roofs or are cream-coloured. While you can hail them in the street, it is usually easier to go to a taxi stand or telephone for one. The majority of taxis are metered. If your taxi doesn't have a meter, make sure you ask what the charge will be before setting out. The starting rate is €1.75 flat charge (which includes first 260 metres) plus €0.05 per 158m thereafter.

Where can I get a taxi?	**Onde posso encontrar um táxi?**
What's the fare to...?	**Quanto custa o percurso para...?**
Where is the nearest railway station/bus stop?	**Onde é a estação ferroviária/ a paragem de autocarros mais próxima?**
When's the next bus/train to...?	**Quando parte o próximo autocarro/comboio para...?**
I want a ticket to...	**Queria um bilhete para...**
single (one-way trip)	**ida**
return (round-trip)	**ida e volta**

first/second class	**primeira/segunda classe**
Will you tell me when to get off?	**Pode dizer-me quando devo descer?**

R

RELIGION

The Portuguese are predominantly Roman Catholic, a fact reflected in surviving religious rituals and saints' days that are public holidays. Services in English are scheduled in principal tourist areas. Protestant (primarily Anglican) services are held in several towns. Full details of all services are available from tourist offices and most hotels; the free monthly *Welcome to the Algarve* also carries an abbreviated listing, and *Algarve Resident* has a full one.

T

TELEPHONE (*telefone*)

Portugal's country code is 351. There are no local dialling codes; you need to dial all 9 digits from anywhere within the country.

White Portugal Telecom public telephones that accept both coins and prepaid telephone cards are found throughout the city. Coin boxes take €0.20, €0.50 and €1.00 coins; unused coins are returned. *Credifone* telephone cards can be purchased at post offices and are much more convenient.

Local, national and international calls can also be made from hotels, but almost always with an exorbitant surcharge. You are wise to make these with an international calling card, if you must make them from your hotel room. (Before departure, be sure to get the international access code in Portugal for your long distance telephone carrier at home.)

To call, pick up the receiver, insert card or coin, wait for the dial tone and dial. To make an international call, dial 00 for an international line (both Europe and overseas; eg. UK 0044, USA 001) + the country code + phone number (including the area code, without the initial '0', where there is one). If you wish to send a fax, you may do so from most hotels, though the charge may seem high.

reverse-charge call	**paga pelo destinatário**
Can you get me this number in …?	**Pode ligar-me para este número em …?**

TIME ZONES *(local)*

Portugal, being at the western edge of Europe, maintains GMT (along with the UK) and is therefore 1 hour behind the rest of the EU. From the last Sunday in March until the last Sunday in October, the clocks are moved one hour ahead for summer time (GMT + 1).

Summer hours:

New York	London	Paris	**Algarve**	Sydney	Auckland
7am	noon	1pm	**noon**	9pm	11pm

What time is it, please? **Que horas são, por favor?**

TIPPING *(serviço; gorjeta)*

Hotel and restaurant bills are generally all-inclusive, but an additional tip of 5–10% is common and even expected in restaurants. Hotel porters, per bag, generally receive €0.50. Give hairdressers, tour guides and taxi drivers around 10%.

TOILETS *(WC; quarto de banho; serviços)*

Public toilets exist in some large towns, but almost every bar and restaurant has one available for public use. Large hotels are also an excellent place to find clean toilets. While it's polite to buy a coffee or drink if you drop in to use the restroom, no one will shout at you for not doing so.

The Ladies' is marked *Senhoras* and the Gentlemen's *Homens*.

Where are the toilets? **Onde são as casas de banho?**

Algarve

TOURIST INFORMATION OFFICES *(turismo)*

Information on the Algarve may be obtained from Portuguese National Tourist Offices (ICEP, or *Investimentos, Comércio e Turismo de Portugal*) in many countries:

Canada: Suite 1005, 60 Bloor Street West, Toronto, Ont. M4W 3B8; Tel. (416) 921 7376.

Ireland: 54 Dawson Street, Dublin. Tel. (353) 1670 9133.

South Africa: 4th floor, Sunnyside Ridge, Sunnyside Drive. PO Box 2473 Houghton, Johannesburg. Tel. (2711) 484 3487.

United Kingdom: 22/25a Sackville St, London W1S 3LY; Tel. (020) 7494 5720.

USA: 590 Fifth Ave, 4th floor, New York, NY 10036; Tel. (212) 354 4403.

In the Algarve itself, all major (and some minor) towns have tourist information offices, staffed by helpful English-speaking assistants. Always make the *turismo* your first stop and pick up the town map/brochure (printed in several languages), which locates all major points of interest. The major Algarve regional office is in Faro (Av. 5 de Outubro, 18; Tel. 289/800 400 or 289/800 477). Others include: Albufeira (Rua 5 de Outubro; Tel. 289/585 279); Lagos (Rua Dr. Vasco da Gama; Tel. 282/763 031); Portimão (Av. Zeca Afonso; Tel. 282/470 732); Praia da Rocha (Av. Tomás Cabreira; Tel. 282/419 132); and Sagres (Rua Comandante Matosos-Vila do Bispo; Tel. 282/624 873). There is also a tourism office in the Faro airport (Tel. 289/818 582).

W

WEBSITES & INTERNET CAFÉS

Websites worth checking before you go include:

<www.portugalvirtual.pt> (general country information and tourism database, with accommodations links)

<www.portugal.org> (the official website of the Portuguese Tourism office)

<www.tap.pt> (the official site of Tap/Air Portugal, the Portuguese national airline)

<www.cp.pt> (site of Caminhos de Ferro Portugueses, national railway network, with timetables and information on international and domestic trains)

<www.rtalgarve.pt> (Algarve region tourism office)

<www.portugalgolf.pt/malis>; <www.golf.pt> (sites on golf, with information specifically related to the Algarve)

<www.pousadas.pt> (Pousadas of Portugal)

Internet cafés: Most resorts have at least one internet café or computer centre where visitors can access e-mail for a small hourly fee. Check with the local tourist information office, as these tend to come and go with regularity. In Albufeiro, visit the Baradoura Internet Café (Urb. Praia de Oura, Loja 5; Tel. 289 592 970).

WEIGHTS & MEASURES

Fluid measures

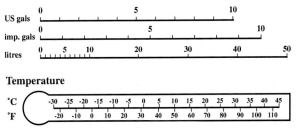

Temperature

125

Algarve

Length

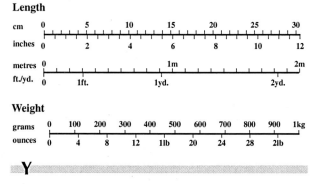

Weight

Y

YOUTH HOSTELS *(pousadas de juventude)*

Four youth hostels operate year-round in the Algarve: at Portimão, Lugar da Coca Maravilhas (Tel. 282/491 804; 180 beds); at Vila Real de Santo António (Rua Dr. Sousa Martins, 40; Tel. 281/544 565; 56 beds); at Alcoutim (Tel. 281/546 004; 54 beds); and at Lagos (Rua de Lançarote de Freitas, 50; Tel. 282/761 970; 62 beds) and at Faro, Rua de PSP – Edifício do IPJ (Tel. 289/826 521; 54 beds).

For additional information, contact the Instituto de Juventude, Rua de PSP, Faro (Tel. 289/891 820), or the headquarters of the Portuguese Youth Hostel Association (Associação Portuguesa de Pousadas de Juventude), Forte Catalezete, Oeiras. Tel. 214/430 638. <www.pousadasjuventude.pt>

Is there a youth hostel near here?

Há alguma pousada de juventude aqui perto?

Recommended Hotels

Visitors have a vast range of accommodation options in this part of Portugal. Hotels are scattered across the major towns and resorts of the Algarve, but densely clustered in sprawling resorts that stretch from Lagos to Faro – especially around Portimão, Albufeira and Vilamoura.

Book well in advance for high season, July–September, when hotel beds are stretched to the limit. Hotel prices are hugely inflated in the height and heat of summer (though many luxury hotels are also at peak rates around Christmas and New Year's). A hotel that is a relative good bargain in May or October – in many ways the best time to visit the Algarve – may be prohibitively overpriced during the summer months.

Room price guidelines below are *rack rates* for a double room with bath in *high* season, including breakfast and VAT (value-added tax). Thus, the prices below may be considerably more than you'll end up paying. All hotels, save for the tiniest residential inns, accept major credit cards. For making reservations, Portugal's country code is 351; the prefixes for the Algarve are 281, 282 and 289 *(see below)*. Hotels are grouped roughly west to east (and in some cases, loosely grouped under subheads).

€€€€€	Very Expensive (above €200)
€€€€	Expensive (€130–200)
€€€	Moderate (€80–130)
€€	Inexpensive (€50–80)
€	Budget (below €50)

SAGRES

Aparthotel Navigator €€€ *Rua Infante D. Henrique, Sagres; Tel. 282/624 354; fax 282/624 360; email <hotel.navigator@mail.telepac.pt>*. This modern hotel, on a cliff right next to the government *pousada*, has basic apartments built around a nice central pool. A good deal for guests who enjoy the low-key, unglitzy appeal of Sagres. Off-season it's an especially good deal. Disabled access. 55 apartments.

Hotel da Baleeira €€–€€€ *Vila de Sagres; Tel. 282/624 212; fax 282/624 425; <www.sagres.net/baleeira>.* A large, good-value hotel overlooking the colourful Sagres harbour and within easy striking distance of several sheltered beaches. Simple rooms, nice pool. Sea-view rooms slightly more expensive. 120 rooms.

Pousada do Infante €€€€ *Ponta da Atalaia, 8650 Sagres; Tel. 282/620 240; fax 282/642 225; <www.pousadas.pt>.* Clinging to a rocky cliff looking out across the Atlantic, this government-owned *pousada* (one of just two along the Algarve) is prized for its location. Rooms are somewhat austere, but most have terraces with excellent views to the coast. Has an annex – a restaurant and small number of rooms – in a medieval fortress, the Fortaleza do Belixe (Tel. 282/624 124). 39 rooms.

LAGOS

Albergaria Casa de São Gonçalo de Lagos €€€ *Rua Cândido dos Reis 73, Lagos; Tel.282/762 171; fax 282/763 927.* This fine 18th-century mansion in the heart of old Lagos has stone staircases that lead to rooms and landings filled with antiques. There is a lovely, plant-ringed interior patio and lounge. Closed in winter. 13 rooms.

Dom Pedro Meia Praia Beach Club €€–€€€ *Meia Praia, Lagos; Tel. 282/780 400; fax 282/780 401; email <algarve.reservations@dompedro.com>.* This large and popular aparthotel is just across the road from one of the longest stretches of sand along the Algarve coast: Meia Praia, the closest beach to Lagos (3 km/ 2 miles) from town. Well-equipped, airy apartments. Two swimming pools, two tennis courts, mini-golf and landscaped gardens. Good roster of activities and golfing discounts. Disabled access. 66 rooms.

Hotel de Lagos €€€€ *Rua Nova da Aldeia, Lagos; Tel. 282/761 020; fax 282/790 345; e-mail <hotel.lagos@mail. telepac.pt>.* An excellent choice for those who would prefer to stay in a hotel with character and style in old Lagos rather than on the beach in a generic seaside hotel. Handsome and colourful rooms, attractive poolside areas, indoor swimming pool, fitness centre, tennis courts, plus water sports at the Duna Beach Club (hotel transport arranged). Disabled access. 319 rooms.

PORTIMÃO/ALVOR/PRAIA DA ROCHA/ TRÊS IRMÃOS

Hotel Bela Vista €€€ *Avenida Tomás Cabreira, Praia da Rocha, Portimão; Tel. 282/450 480; fax 282/415 369.* The first hotel in the Algarve, this free-standing mansion overlooks the beach and looks wholly out-of-place on very built-up Praia da Rocha. This architectural gem, resembling a church more than a hotel, was built as a summer house in 1916. Its interior features beautiful wood ceilings and staircases, plus splendid 19th-century *azulejos*. First-floor rooms have large balconies; only two rooms, less desirable, have views of the unattractive beach town at the back. 14 rooms.

Hotel Carvoeiro Sol €€€€ *Praia do Carvoeiro, Lagoa; Tel. 282/357 301; fax 282/357 211; e-mail <carvoeirosol@mail. telepac.pt>.* Wedged right into the narrow opening between twin cliffs above Carvoeiro's tiny beach, this modern, comfortable hotel has a central courtyard, bar and restaurant, and clean, bright, beach-style rooms. Disabled access. 54 rooms.

Hotel Dom João II €€€–€€€€ *Praia de Alvor, (1 km/ 0.6 miles from Alvor), Tel. 282/400 700; fax 282/400 799; <www. pestana.com>.* A Pestana group hotel, this 7-story complex is bright and airy with a large swimming pool and spacious sun terraces. Some rooms have sea views. A short walk from a tranquil beach. Part of the expansive Torralta tourist complex, which offers a wide range of sporting facilities, shopping and entertainment possibilities. 219 rooms.

Hotel Oriental €€€€ *Avenida Tomás Cabreira, Praia da Rocha, Portimão; Tel. 282/480 000; fax 282/413 413.* In the more upscale (and slightly more tranquil) end of Praia da Rocha, this Moorish fantasy palace was designed in the style of the casino that stood on this spot in the 1920s. Features a galleried interior, Turkish bath, pretty gardens with sun terraces, and swimming pools looking onto the beach. Disabled access. 85 rooms.

Le Méridien Penina €€€€–€€€€€ *Montes de Alvor, Portimão; Tel. 282/420 200. Fax. 282/420 300. email <reservations@lemeridien-algarve.com>.* The original luxury golf resort on the Algarve is set within a 360-acre estate, which includes the world-famous Penina golf course. Perfect for the well-heeled sports lover, with floodlit tennis, sailing, windsurfing, horseback riding and gym. 196 rooms.

Pestana Alvor Praia Hotel €€€€€ *Praia de Três Irmãos, Alvor; Tel. 282/400 900; fax 282/400 999; e-mail <reservas. algarve@pestana.com>.* This large and luxurious, recently refurbished hotel sits among thick trees and gardens on cliffs. It overlooks one of the finest beaches along the coast, Praia de Três Irmãos, floodlit at night. Olympic-size seawater pool with ocean views. Three top-flight restaurants with terraces and different cuisines. Tennis courts, full spa. Disabled access. 198 rooms.

Residencial Praia do Vau €€ *Portimão; Tel. 282/401 312; fax 282/401 756.* A small, rustic and comfortable inn in an attractive Algarvian house just 200 m (650 ft) from the Praia do Vau beach (west of Praia da Rocha). 21 rooms.

Residencial Solar do Penguim € *Avenida Tomás Cabreira, Portimão; Tel./fax 282/424 308.* This 75-year-old private house with an even older proprietor enjoys a magnificent location with the best possible vista of the main beach from its terraces. Charming Old World atmosphere, but best for the adventurous. Reservations by fax preferred. 13 rooms.

MONCHIQUE

Estalagem Abrigo da Montanha €€–€€€ *Estrada Monchique-Fóia, Monchique; Tel. 282/912 131; fax 282/913 660; e-mail <abrigodamontanha@hotmail.com>*. High up in the Serra de Monchique, away from the heat and crowds of the coast, this wood-and-granite mountain lodge is a special retreat. It's not luxurious, but it has style and spectacular views. Pretty rooftop pool and café-restaurant across the road. Slightly more expensive rooms are larger with a bigger terrace. 16 rooms.

ALBUFEIRA/FALÉSIA

Albufeira Jardim I & II €€ *Cerro da Piedade, Albufeira; Tel. 289/570 070/090; fax 289/570 071*. A large enclosed complex of whitewashed tourist apartments sit on a hill overlooking the sea. They enjoy fine views and a quiet setting, only a 5-minute walk into town. With 5 pools, tennis courts, shopping, bars and supermarket. All apartments have either a balcony or terrace. Good value. Bus shuttle service to beach and Albufeira town. 470 apartments.

Alfagar Aldeamento Turístico €€€ *Balaia, Albufeira; Tel. 289/540 220; fax 289/542 770; <www.alfagar.com>*. Very nicely landscaped gardens and a cliff-top walkway surround this good-value holiday apartment complex. One-, two- and three-bedroom apartments with cleaning service five days a week. Just a short walk to the beaches on either side. 220 apartments.

Hotel Apartamentos Ourapraia/Clube Praia da Oura €€€ *Areias São João, Albufeira; Tel. 289/590 326; fax 289/585 288; e-mail <reservas@clubepraiadaoura. com>*. A very attractive holiday complex of cute, well-equipped apartments centred around equally agreeable pools. Tennis courts, sauna and close proximity to the Albufeira beach. Excellent value, especially during high season. 126 apartments.

Hotel Boa Vista €€€ *Rua Samora Barros 20, Albufeira; Tel. 289/589 175; fax 289/589 180; e-mail <hotelboavista@hoteisbelver.pt>.* Superb setting, built into the cliff at the very western end of town, with a view over the whole of Albufeira. Close enough to walk to town but far enough away to be quiet in high season. Swimming pool and sun terrace. 93 rooms.

Hotel Falésia €€€ *Pinhal do Concelho, Praia da Falésia; Tel. 289/501 237; fax 289/501 270; <www.falesia.com>.* A modern hotel that looks like an apartment building on the edge of the Pine Cliffs resort and golf course. Garden-like lobby, pool with waterfall, some 1- and 2-bedroom apartments. Falésia beach access is through adjacent Sheraton. Disabled access. 145 rooms.

Hotel Sol e Mar €–€€ *Rua José Bernadino de Sousa, Albufeira; Tel. 289/580 080; fax 289/587 036; e-mail <hotelsolmar@ mail.telepac.pt>.* A large block hotel in the town centre with somewhat dated rooms but good value given its main asset – it's built right into the cliff on Albufeira's desirable beach. Indoor pool. A popular economy package-tour hotel. 74 rooms.

Residencial Villa Recife €–€€ *Rua Miguel Bombarda, 6, Albufeira; Tel. 289/583 740; fax 289/587 182.* A two-minute walk from the heart of old Albufeira, a converted private house with a pleasant garden entrance. The old section of the house has more character than the modern wing. 91 rooms.

Sheraton Algarve (Pine Cliffs) Hotel & Resort €€€€€ *Praia da Falésia, Albufeira; Tel. 289/500 100; fax 289/501 950;*

<*www. luxurycollection.com*>. One of the Algarve's most distin-guished and luxurious developments, surrounded by pines at the top of dramatic cliffs. Handsome Moorish styling, excellent restau-rants and extensive sporting facilities, including 9-hole cliff-top golf course, tennis, semi-private beach, 3 pools and spa. Brand-new luxury 'Golf Suites', plus villas and apartments. Great facilities for children. Disabled access. 215 rooms (33 suites, 70 apartments).

Vila Channa €€€ *São Rafael, Albufeira; Tel. 289/592 354; fax 289/591 597*. A nice, clean, villa-style small hotel a short walk from a couple of the prettiest beaches near Albufeira, Castelo and São Rafael. Nice pool. 18 rooms.

Vila Joya €€€€ *Praia da Galé, Albufeira; Tel. 289/591 795; fax 289/591 201; email <vila.joya@clix.pt>*. Probably the most styl-ish hotel on the entire coast, this sumptuously decorated small palazzo is full year-round. Ensconced in beautiful gardens, the Moorish-influenced villa is just minutes from the pretty, calm Galé beach. Beautiful baths and public rooms. Most rooms have sea views. Lovely small pool. Reserve several months in advance. 17 rooms.

VILAMOURA

Dom Pedro Marina €€€€ *Avenida Tivoli Lote H4, Vilamoura, Quarteira; Tel. 289/381 000; fax 289/381 001; <www. dompedro. com>*. Impressive hotel with a tropical feel – palm trees, wicker furniture, tile floors and bamboo shades – perched right on the edge of the Vilamoura marina. Nice gardens and pool. Preferential terms for guests at local golf courses. Disabled access. 262 rooms.

Tivoli Marinhotel €€€€€ *Vilamoura; Tel. 289/303 303; fax 289/303 345; <www.tivolihotels.com>*. Sandwiched between the marina and the beach, this hotel is the perfect metaphor for Vilamoura resort: massive, slick and expensive. Like the resort, though, it also completes its aims very well. Great views, ultramodern lobby, very good restaurants, state-of-the-art facilities, tennis courts and indoor and outdoor pools to pamper guests. Disabled access. 389 rooms.

VALE DO LOBO/QUINTA DO LAGO

Hotel Quinta do Lago €€€€€ *Quinta do Lago, Almancil; Tel. 289/350 350; fax 289/396 393; <www.quintadolagohotel. com>.* One of the standard bearers for luxury and leisure in the Algarve, this Orient Express hotel is set amidst almost 2,000 acres of gardens and woods. Rooms are tastefully and elegantly decorated. Three golf courses wend their fairways through the Ria Formosa Nature Preserve and are among the finest in Europe. Watersports, health club, pools and beach access across lovely wooden bridge. Distinguished service. Disabled access. 141 rooms.

Le Méridien Dona Filipa €€€€€ *Vale do Lobo, Tel. 289/357 200; fax 289/357 201.* A handsomely appointed hotel that's a favourite of Algarve golfers. Set amidst 450 acres, part of the exclusive Vale do Lobo resort, it has elegant traditional rooms and public areas, plus a gambling room. Green fees at the excellent San Lorenzo golf course included. 3 floodlit tennis courts. Good golf packages available. Disabled access. 147 rooms.

FARO

Hotel Eva €€€ *Avenida da República, 1, Faro; Tel. 289/803 354; fax 289/802 304.* The biggest hotel in Faro, the fort-like Eva, was refurbished in the mid-1990s. A large, modern block on the edge of the harbour 90 metres (100 yards) from pedestrian shopping streets and the old town. Several bars and restaurants, a disco and folklore shows. Disabled access. 150 rooms.

Hotel Faro €€€ *Praça Dom F. Gomes, 2, Faro; Tel. 289/830 830; fax 289/830 829.* This formerly pleasant hotel was revamped from the ground up in 2000. Now part of Faro's swankiest shopping centre, the hotel is ideally placed – just outside the old town and overlooking a lively plaza and the harbour – and appealingly chic. Disabled access. 52 rooms.

SÃO BRÁS DE ALPORTEL

Pousada de São Brás €€€ *São Brás de Alportel; Tel. 289/842 305; fax 289/841 726; <www.pousadas.pt>.* A quiet manor house *pousada* with views of both surrounding mountains and the sea a half hour away. This was the first *pousada* built in the Algarve, in 1942, and the second in all Portugal. A good place to get away from the sunbathing masses to relax. 41 rooms.

TAVIRA

Casa do Rio €€ *Estrada da Asseca, Tavira; Tel. 281/326 578.* Nice bed & breakfast in a private home with a pool right on the river in historic Tavira. 5 rooms.

O Pequeno Castelo € *Poço das Bruxas, Santo Estavão, Tavira; Tel./fax 281/961 692.* On the outskirts of picturesque Tavira, a quiet and friendly bed & breakfast inn with views of the Atlantic from the veranda. Well placed for walks in the countryside. Pool. Minimum stay of 4 nights. 4 rooms and apartment (on request).

Convento de São António €€ *Atalaia 56, Tavira; Tel./fax 281/325 632.* This small, family-owned guesthouse was a monastery in the 17th century. The elegantly appointed rooms are certainly much more comfortable than they once were as monks' cells. Nice swimming pool and central patio. Minimum stay required. 7 rooms.

Recommended Restaurants

For most visitors, dining in the Algarve is still limited to hotel food and the occasional café-snack bar in town or on the beach. There are plenty of very good restaurants in the major towns and resorts, but there are also many that seem far more intent on separating tourists from their euros than offering genuine Algarvian and Portuguese food. The guide below should help you find more authentic eating experiences.

The prices indicated are for starter, main course and dessert, with wine, per person. (Note that some fish or shellfish dishes, charged by the kilo, will be more expensive than the averages.) Service and VAT of 12% are included, as they generally are in the bill. Except where noted, all restaurants accept major credit cards.

Prices normally include taxes and a service charge, but it is customary to leave an additional 5–10% tip for good service.

€€€€	Very Expensive (over €40)
€€€	Expensive (€25–40)
€€	Moderate (€15–25)
€	Inexpensive (below €15)

SAGRES

Fortaleza do Belixe €€€ *Fortaleza do Beliche (5km/3 miles east of Sagres); Tel. 282/624 124.* Open daily for lunch and dinner. This formal restaurant in a medieval fortress (an annex of the *pousada* in Sagres) is perhaps best recommended for its décor, which aims to give visitors a dose of Portugal's past navigational glories. It serves decent regional cooking.

Restaurante Tasca €€–€€€ *Porto de Sagres; Tel. 282/624 177.* Open daily for lunch and dinner. This restaurant is one of the best in Sagres for fresh seafood. Choose to dine on the sun-scorched outdoor terrace that overlooks the harbour or in the dark stone interior. Both serve the same great sea bass, lobster and grilled squid kebabs.

Vila Velha €€–€€€ *Ponta da Atalaia; Tel. 282/624 788.* Open Tues–Sun for lunch and dinner. Just down the road from the *pousada*, the husband-and-wife team that operates this attractive rustic restaurant serve well-prepared, large portions of traditional Portuguese dishes. The daily *ementa*, or fixed-price menu, for two is a good deal.

LAGOS

Cervejaria-Grill Arribalé €€ *Rua da Barroca, 40; Tel. 282/761 303.* Open Tues–Sun for lunch and dinner. This cute, tiny tavern specialises in fresh grilled fish. There are only a few tables inside, but customers spill out on to a narrow street in the old quarter.

Dom Sebastião €€€ *Rua 25 de Abril 20–22; Tel. 282/762 795.* Open daily for lunch and dinner (closed Sun in winter). On Lagos's main pedestrian thoroughfare, this very popular, rustic-style restaurant with dark beams focuses on live seafood. It also has outdoor tables.

Escondidinho €–€€ *Beco do Cemitério; Tel. 282/760 386.* Open Mon–Sat for lunch and dinner. A typical, family restaurant where grilled fish is the speciality, and the cooking is done in front of the customers. Traditional *cataplanas* (fish or meat) are also recommended.

A Lagosteira €€ *Rua 1 Maio, 20; Tel. 282/762 486.* Open daily except lunch Sat and Sun. This long-established simple restaurant is centrally located and serves good, imaginative seafood. The fish *cataplana* is particularly good. Some outdoor tables.

MONCHIQUE–FÓIA

Abrigo da Montanha €€–€€€ *Estrada da Fóia; Tel. 282/912 131.* Open daily for lunch and dinner. One of several good roadside restaurants with terraces enjoying panoramic views. Try the *frango piri-piri* (spicy chicken), which comes in mountainous portions to echo the view; or the *cataplana*.

PORTIMÃO

A Lanterna €€ *Portimão Bridge (Ferragudo side); Tel. 282/ 414 429.* Open Mon–Sat for dinner. This long-established restaurant has a reputation for high quality, with elegant dining in small, traditionally furnished rooms. Specials include smoked fish and some interesting desserts.

Restaurante Dona Barca €–€€ *Largo da Barca; Tel. 282/484 189.* Open daily for lunch and dinner. This fish restaurant has an excellent reputation for quality fresh food and typical Algarvian cuisine – it has even represented the region at various national gastronomic festivals. The dining room is pleasant, with stone walls and draped fishing nets.

PRAIA DA ROCHA

A Casa da Rocha €€–€€€ *Sítio dos Castelos, Av. Tomás Cabreira; Tel. 282/419 674.* If it's a restaurant with a view you're after, you could hardly do better than this place, in an airy summer beach house with three terraces and consummate panoramic views of the ocean. Sunset dinners are understandably popular. Choose from Portuguese tapas and grilled fish and meats.

Penguin Terrace € *Avenida Tomás Cabreira (next to Residencial Solar Pinguim), Tel. 282/424 308.* Open Mon–Sat for lunch and dinner. Halfway down the steps to the beach, this cute terrace restaurant is perfect for a beachside snack and an informal evening meal of homecooked food. Try the grilled chicken *piri-piri,* any of the blackboard specials or the excellent salads. Friendly staff, lively atmosphere and beach views. No credit cards.

Churrasqueira da Rocha €€€ *Avenida Tomás Cabreira; Tel. 282/417 452.* Open daily for lunch and dinner. *Churrasqueira* means grill, and you can get lots of grilled meats – including the famous *espetadas*, or kebabs – and the house speciality, chicken *piri-piri*, at this large place with good views of the beach.

Safari €–€€ *Rua António Feu; Tel. 282/423 540.* Open daily for lunch and dinner. This sea-view restaurant combines good Portuguese cuisine with a distinctive Angolan flavour (carried over into the décor). Don't be put off by the name – the food is good value and different.

PRAIA DE TRES IRMÃOS/ALVOR

Restaurante Ababuja €€–€€€ *Rua da Ribeira; Tel. 282/458 979.* Open daily for lunch and dinner (except Wed lunch). Situated on the waterfront, near the fish market, this family-run restaurant has simple décor and friendly service. Not surprisingly, it's well known for its fresh fish and seafood but does unusual specialities including stuffed squid and cuttlefish with beans. The catch of the day is always a good bet.

Búzios €€€ *Aldeamento Turístico de Prainha, Praia de Tres Irmãos; Tel. 282/458 772.* Open daily for dinner. Ensconced in a beach community of white houses and condos, a short walk up from the beach, this chic restaurant has an appealing terrace and international menu (including traditional Portuguese cuisine). Good wine list.

ALBUFEIRA

A Ruina €€–€€€ *Cais Herculano, Tel. 289/512 094.* Open daily for lunch and dinner. A 19th-century, four-story mansion, 'the Ruin' features a basic dining room downstairs, rustic-looking restaurant on the second floor and roof-top dining with views over Praia dos Pescadores. Suitable for a place near the fish market and just west of 'Fishermen's beach', the speciality is well-prepared seafood. Try the *caldeirada* (fish stew).

Restaurante do Hotel Vila Joya €€€€ *in Hotel Vila Joya, Praia de Galé; Tel. 289/591 795.* Open daily for lunch and dinner; closed from mid-Nov–Mar. The restaurant of the most luxurious and sumptuously designed small hotel along the Algarve is, like the hotel, refined and elegant. To suit its multi-national patrons, the kitchen prepares eclectic international dishes. Reservations for non-guests essential.

La Cigale €€€ *Praia de Olhos d'Água, Tel. 289/501 637.* Open daily for lunch and dinner. Excellent seafood in a rustic, white-washed beachside restaurant with an attractive terrace. Perfect for lazy and informal eating by day, La Cigale is elegant and romantic by night. Try the *mollusc a la cigale*, a shellfish special. Other favourites include fondues and *cataplana*.

Restaurante Marisqueira €€€ *Praia de Santa Eulália; Tel. 289/542 636.* Open daily for lunch and dinner. If you arrive early for lunch or dinner, you'll be rewarded with a window seat and excellent views over Santa Eulália beach to accompany quality Algarvian cooking. Fresh fish and seafood specialities.

NEAR ALMANCIL

Casa Velha €€€€ *Quinta do Lago, Almancil; Tel. 289/394 983.* Open Mon–Sat for dinner. The elegant resort that's grown up around it has only recently caught up to the chic standards set by this restaurant for nearly three decades. In a renovated 19th-century farmhouse (hence the name, 'old house'), this is about as elegant as dining in the Algarve gets. The French menu is sophisticated, the dishes artfully prepared and the service perfect, but it's not at all stuffy. Excellent wine cellar.

Restaurante Ermitage €€€€ *Estrada Almancil-Vale do Lobo; Tel. 289/394 329.* Open Tues–Sun for dinner. The Dutch duo behind this ancient farmhouse-turned-elegant-restaurant have created a treat for their international clientele of expatriates and upscale visitors to the Quinta do Lago and Vale do Lobo resort area. The creative menu, which uses the freshest ingredients, changes seasonally.

Gigi Beach €€€ *Quinta do Lago; Tel. 09/404 5178.* Open daily for lunch. The setting is simple: a wooden beach shack tucked in among the dunes and wetlands of the Ria Formosa Nature Preserve, reached across a long wooden bridge. The food is also simple: point to the fresh-caught fish of your choice and watch it taken direct to the grill.

Pequeno Mundo €€€ *Pereiras (Almancil, just off Estrada de Quarteira) Tel. 289/399 866.* Open Mon–Sat for dinner. In a charming setting of renovated cottages, gourmet-standard French and international cuisine is prepared by an English proprietor. Don't miss out on the delicious fig and almond frangipane tart. Terrace and indoor dining.

VILAMOURA

Restaurante O Cesteiro €€€ *Estrada de Falésia-Vilamoura; Tel. 289/312 961.* Open Thur–Tues for lunch and dinner. This terrace restaurant overlooks the glittering Vilamoura marina, so you can ponder the yachts as you sample charcoal-grilled fish and seafood items.

Restaurante Pier One €€€ *Clube Náutico, Marina da Vilamoura; Tel. 289/322 734.* Open daily for lunch and dinner. With a terrace that offers panoramic views of the marina and, in the distance, the sea, Pier One is a tempting place for alfresco dining at sunset. Interesting selections, such as

Algarve

Mozambican prawns, monkfish lasagna and chicken, and bananas in a puff pastry.

FARO

Restaurante Mesa dos Mouros €€–€€€ *Largo da Sé; Tel. 289/878 873.* Open daily for lunch and dinner. A cute place with a nice platform terrace in the shadow of the cathedral in the heart of Faro's old town, 'Table of the Moors' is a good place for a sightseeing break during the day and a simple lunch of grilled sardines.

Dois Irmãos €€ *Largo do Terreiro do Bispo 18, Tel. 289/823 337.* The Two Brothers restaurant has been a Faro seafood legend since as long ago as 1925. This simple bistro has an extensive fish menu, including nine types of *cataplana*, and lots of regional specials.

Taska €€–€€€ *Rua do Alportel, 38; Tel. 289/824 739.* Open Mon–Sat for lunch and dinner. This small simple restaurant serves unusual and authentic Algarvian fare. There's also an excellent selection of wines.

TAVIRA

Quatro Águas €€€ *Sítio das Quatro Aguas; Tel. 281/325 329.* Open daily for lunch and dinner; winter, closed Mon. This handsome 18th-century building on the harbour is a fine choice for a seafood meal. Traditional Portuguese dining, with an emphasis on dishes such as *arroz de marisco* (seafood rice), *cataplana* and octopus chowder.

INDEX